Scholastic Environmental Atlas of the United States

Illustrations: Moffitt Cecil; concept and design, Helen Driggs.

Maps: Christopher Salvatico

Photos: cover photo credits from top left to right: Myrleen Ferguson Cate/Photo Edit, Ron Levy, Peter Brandt, Wayne Eastep, Robert Llewellyn, Letraset Phototone™, Baron Wolman. pp. 8, Myrleen Ferguson/PhotoEdit; 9, Tony Freeman/ PhotoEdit; 21, 23, 42, 44 (top), 65, Mark Mattson; 22, F. Sieb/ H. Armstrong Roberts; 24, 27 (bot.), U.S. Forest Service; 27 (top), Stephen McBrady/PhotoEdit; 28 (top), 32 (top), 60, Robert Mason; 28 (bot.), M. Schneiders/H. Armstrong Roberts; 29, U.S. Fish and Wildlife Service/Randy Wilk; 30, H. Abernathy/ H. Armstrong Roberts; 34, Soil Conservation Service/Tim McCabe; 36, Urban Archives; 37 (top), C.T. Delamo/ H. Armstrong Roberts; 37 (bot.), M. Berman/H. Armstrong Roberts; 41 (left), Carnegie Library, Pittsburgh; 41 (right), John A. Wee; 43, Myrleen Ferguson Cate/PhotoEdit; 44 (bot.), M. Thonig/H. Armstrong Roberts; 51, Larry Lee/H. Armstrong Roberts; 55, R. Krubner/H. Armstrong Roberts; 57, M. Roessler/H. Armstrong Roberts; 61,W. Bertsch/H. Armstrong Roberts.

LIBRARY OF CONGRESS CATALOGING-IN-PUBLICATION DATA

Mattson, Mark T.
    The Scholastic environmental atlas of the United States / Mark Mattson.
        p.   cm.

    Includes bibliographical references, glossary, and index.

    ISBN 0-590-49354-X : $14.95. -- ISBN 0-590-49355-8 (pbk.) : $7.95

    1. Nature conservation -- United States -- Maps.
2. Pollution -- Environmental aspects -- United States -- Maps.
3. Man -- Influence on nature -- United States -- Maps.
4. Natural resources -- United States -- Maps   I. Title   II. Title: Environmental atlas of the United States.

G1201.G3M35   1993   <G&M>
333.7'0973'022—dc20   92–46757
                                                    CIP
                                            MAP AC

12 11 10 9 8 7 6 5 4 3 2 1   3 4 5 6 7 8/9

Printed in the U.S.A.
First Scholastic printing, August 1993

Scholastic Environmental Atlas of the United States

Mark Mattson

Scholastic
Reference

SCHOLASTIC INC.

New York   Toronto   London   Auckland   Sydney

Contents

Introduction

The United States possesses many of our planet's riches—fertile soils, dense forests, fresh water, and abundant wildlife. The United States also has environmental problems. Water pollution, acid rain, and wetland destruction are just some of the important issues that our nation faces. This atlas looks both at our land's great resources and the threats to them.

The earth has changed countless times in its four and one-half billion years. It has evolved into a special place that supports life unlike any other place that we know of in the universe. During the earth's history, many animals and plants have come and gone. Many of the kinds of animals that we know today did not exist a few thousand years ago. Human beings, as *homo sapiens,* have only come to our planet within the last 40,000 years.

Human Changes. Despite our "recent" arrival on earth, humans have changed the environment more than any other living thing. With our ability to think and use tools, we have reworked the planet to make it more comfortable for ourselves and our communities. In the United States, our high standard of living has been built on the use of our great and bountiful natural resources.

Many of the changes that people have made have created difficulties for the plants, animals, and, even people, who live here. Cars, highways, cities, and irrigation are just a few cases of human inventions that pose threats to other living things. This atlas shows how these changes have affected our fellow creatures and their habitats.

We have always counted on the earth to adapt to our changes and repair itself no matter what we did to it. But lately we have come to realize that this planet, too, is alive and has needs. Our air, land, and water resources need our care and protection. This atlas also shows how we can make changes to help restore nature's balance.

Using This Book. Like all atlases, this book has many maps. Each of these maps will give you information about some aspect of the environment in the United States. You don't have to read it from beginning to end. You can look up the topics that most interest you.

The map on the next page shows the environmental quality in every state. It shows how each state measures up on issues like air and

Environmental problems aren't always huge oil spills or buried toxic wastes. Many are as simple as trash that has been thoughtlessly thrown on the street or in an open field.

water quality, the disposal of dangerous wastes, and passing laws to clean up the environment. Throughout this book we use maps to show locations and amounts of resources, as well as sources of different kinds of pollution.

Many of the photographs in this book reflect what a beautiful country we live in, and how that environment has changed over time. The drawings and diagrams show processes that you cannot see on a map or in a photograph. Through all these illustrations, you can get a clear picture of the environment of the United States.

Our Job. The United States is one of the earth's most gifted countries. We have a responsibility to use its resources wisely. Only recently have people in the United States become really aware of our environment. We have discovered many problems. But we must not stop there.

Our planet needs the efforts of each of us to become safe and healthy again. There are many different ways to lend a hand to the planet. Some of you may even grow up to be environmental scientists or teachers. All of us can help take better care of the earth and its resources.

This book will give you some ideas. The rest is up to you.

Even the smallest kids can make a big impact on the environment. To make things better, we can educate ourselves and get involved.

How Does Your State Rate on Environmental Issues?

Map Key

- Not good
- Good
- Average
- Very good

Ecosystems

About 200 million years ago, the seven continents of the earth were linked together in the center of one large ocean. They formed a giant continent that stretched from the North Pole far into the Southern Hemisphere. Scientists today call this great continent Pangaea.

Continental Drift. What caused this great landmass to separate? Pangaea sat on giant plates of rock that form the earth's crust. Underneath, boiling rock, called **magma,** created pressure. The force of the explosive magma very slowly pushed the continents apart, separating Pangaea. Over hundreds of thousands of years, the continents drifted in different directions. Oceans filled the spaces between them.

New Environments. Like giant puzzle pieces, the once-linked parts of Pangaea contained common plants and animals. But as the continents came apart, living things were left

stranded, separated by large oceans. Some had to survive in tropical rainforests as they drifted towards the Equator. Others had to withstand icy temperatures as they moved toward polar regions. In order to live, plants and animals had to adapt. They changed their forms to cope with their new surroundings. These changes made them different from related species on other continents.

PANGAEA

Europe • Asia • North America • Africa • South America • Australia • Antarctica

200 Million BC

Shifting Continents

Africa fit perfectly between North and South America 200 million years ago. Now, Africa is 3700 miles from the East Coast of the United States. This distance increases about two inches every year.

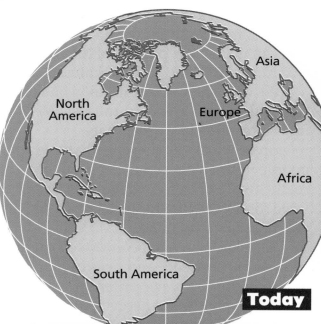

Asia • North America • Europe • Africa • South America

Today

The Drifting Continents

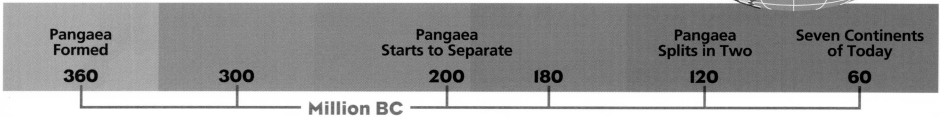

Pangaea Formed		Pangaea Starts to Separate		Pangaea Splits in Two	Seven Continents of Today
360	300	200	180	120	60

— **Million BC** —

Land-shaping Forces

Natural forces like ice, fire, and wind have shaped the face of the United States. In the center of the country, flatlands stretch out into grassy prairies. In the West, ranges of high, sharp mountains form a rocky spine north to south. In the East, a gently rolling plain slopes from Appalachia into the Atlantic Ocean.

The special features of the earth, like mountains, river valleys, or canyons, are called **landforms.** Landforms can be created by forces at work on the earth's surface like erosion or the movement of glaciers. Landforms can result also from movement or pressure underneath the earth's crust. Each of these forces individually can change the earth, or they can work together. The changes may happen in an instant, or over thousands of years.

Wear and Tear. When soil is carried away by wind or water, the effect is called **erosion.** Sometimes, the eroded soil is carried many miles away from its starting point. Erosion can happen very slowly—the Grand Canyon took millions of years to form—or it can happen very fast. In the mountain and desert areas of the West, flash floods sometimes erode tons of soil in several minutes. Homes, streets, and even neighborhoods may wash away.

The Power of Ice. Glaciers, great

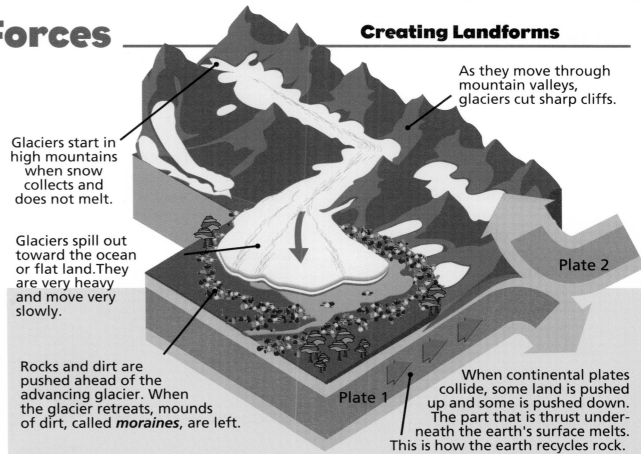

Glaciers start in high mountains when snow collects and does not melt.

As they move through mountain valleys, glaciers cut sharp cliffs.

Glaciers spill out toward the ocean or flat land. They are very heavy and move very slowly.

Rocks and dirt are pushed ahead of the advancing glacier. When the glacier retreats, mounds of dirt, called *moraines*, are left.

Plate 1

Plate 2

When continental plates collide, some land is pushed up and some is pushed down. The part that is thrust underneath the earth's surface melts. This is how the earth recycles rock.

masses of ice and snow, work like sandpaper, scraping the countryside flat. As they move, glaciers bulldoze the land, picking up rocks and scraping the soil beneath them. When glaciers melt, they leave dirt and rocks behind in piles called **moraines.** The town of Moraine in Ohio is named for a glacial deposit. Glaciers exert a tremendous force on the land, digging chunks from the earth as they pass. When glaciers melt, these holes fill with water, forming lakes. The hundreds of lakes in Montana's Glacier

National Park were created this way.

Shifting Plates. The solid plates under the earth's surface are under great pressure. As a result they sometimes move or shift. We can see and feel this movement in earthquakes and volcanoes that tear the land and cause great destruction. But the movement of plates also builds up the earth. The Rocky Mountains were formed when two plates crashed into each other, thrusting some land into the air and other land beneath the rocky crust.

Soils

The rich farm dirt of Illinois, the mud of the Mississippi Delta, and the shifting dunes of the Mojave Desert are all part of the earth's covering called **soil.** Soil is made up of crushed rock and broken down parts of plants and animals. It forms a loose covering on top of the earth's rocky crust. Without soil, plants would not be able to take root or flower. Animals would have no place to graze or burrow. Humans would not be able to grow food or eat.

Color Clues. Soils come in a variety of colors, depending on what materials they contain. Reddish-orange soils are made from rock that is rich in iron. Jet-black soils are filled with decaying plants and dead animals.

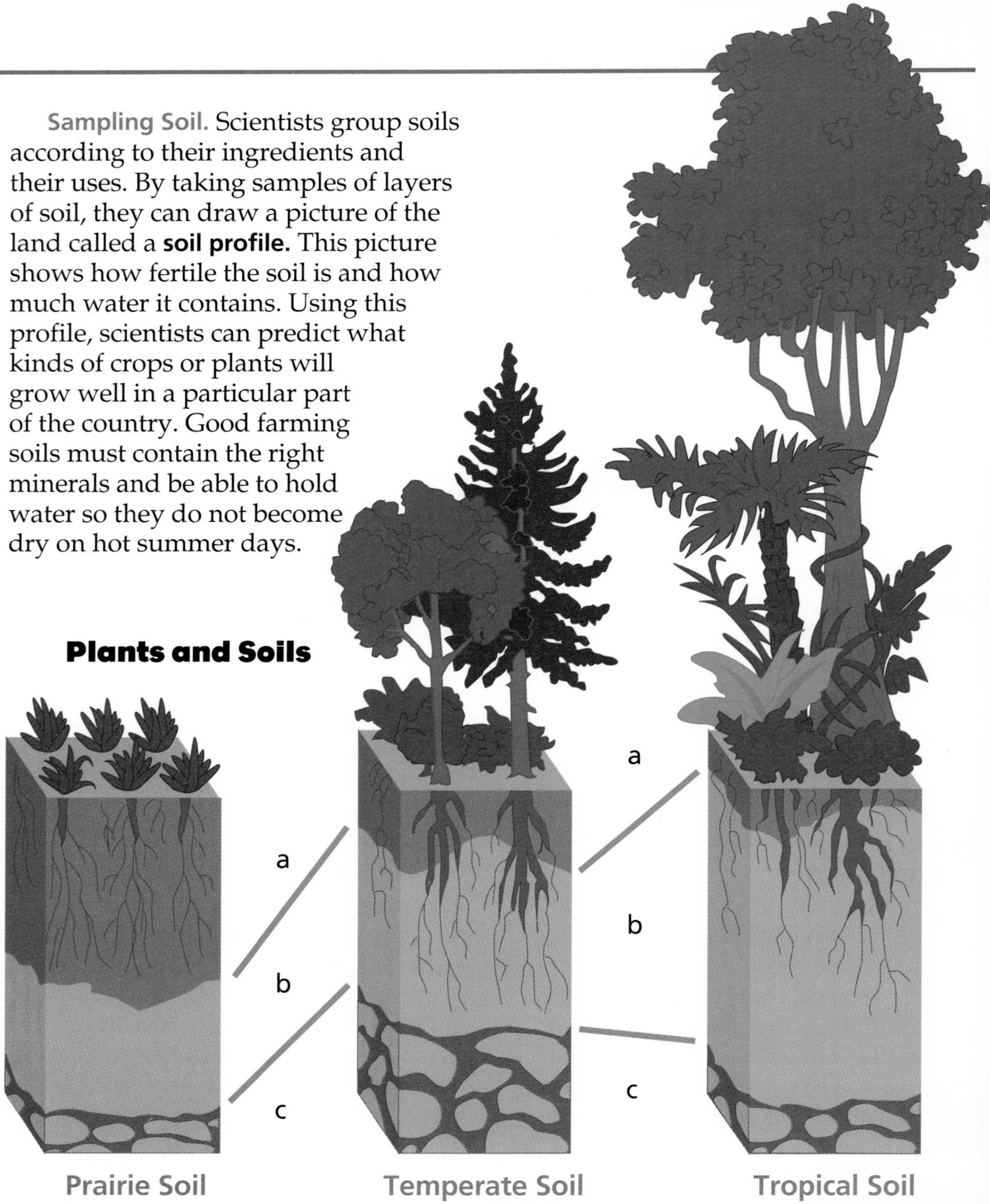

Plants need soil for water, food, and minerals. They grow roots to reach the layer of soil with the right conditions. Soil collects water and keeps it from evaporating. Some soil, like clay, is dense and can hold water for a long time. If soil is sandy, water runs quickly through it. Soil provides plants with organic food from decaying plants and animals plus minerals from ash and bits of rock. The "a" layer of these soil profiles is organic. The "b" layer is mostly organic but contains some rock. The "c" layer is bedrock that lies under the soil.

Sampling Soil. Scientists group soils according to their ingredients and their uses. By taking samples of layers of soil, they can draw a picture of the land called a **soil profile.** This picture shows how fertile the soil is and how much water it contains. Using this profile, scientists can predict what kinds of crops or plants will grow well in a particular part of the country. Good farming soils must contain the right minerals and be able to hold water so they do not become dry on hot summer days.

Plants and Soils

a

b

c

a

b

c

a

b

c

Prairie Soil

Temperate Soil

Tropical Soil

Alaska

Arctic
Arctic soils are thin and light in color. These soils, and the water they hold, are frozen for many months of the year. Because the soil is so cold, things cannot easily decay in it. Arctic soils contain many bits of stone and rock that have broken apart in the icy temperatures.

Mountain
Mountain soils are filled with rocks and stones that were pushed up from underneath the earth's surface. They are usually thin, and gray or light brown in color. These soils are often eroded by water flowing down the mountainside.

Desert
Desert soils are often coarse. They contain lots of minerals. Little vegetation can survive in these soils because they do not hold enough water. But they can be used for farming if they are irrigated.

Prairie
Prairie soils are brown, dense, and very fertile. Tall grasses that naturally grow in these soils put down deep, thick roots that can survive when droughts make the land completely dry. Great crops of corn and wheat grow in prairie soil.

Nine Soils of the United States

Glacial
Glacial soils were pushed down from Canada by glaciers during the last ice age. They are mostly brown and stoney. Some glacial soil has been enriched by grassland cover and is good for farming. Other glacial soils must be fertilized to grow crops.

Wetland
Wetland soils are often rinsed of nutrients by the water that surrounds them. The constant decay of plants and animals replenishes these soils, however, and they are good for growing crops. They are dark brown and very dense.

Hawaii

Tropical
Tropical soils are dark and wet. Hawaii has the only true tropical soils in the United States. Although tropical soils are not always very fertile, those in Hawaii are enriched with ash from volcanoes which makes them excellent for farming.

0   200   400
Miles

River
River, or alluvial, soils are rich and fine-grained. They are formed from eroded topsoil carried along by the flow of water. They contain many minerals and are very fertile.

Temperate
Temperate soils are found in many parts of the country. Most farmers grow their crops in this loose, brown, and fertile soil.

Water Cycles

The mighty Mississippi, the Great Lakes, and countless other rivers, lakes, and streams make up the water cover of the United States. What few people realize, though, is that twice as much water is stored underneath the ground. This water is held naturally in cavities called **aquifers.** The water Americans use every day comes from all of these sources. In urban areas, water supplies are stored in holding areas called **reservoirs.**

The Water Cycle. The water in earth's atmosphere condenses in the sky, falls to the ground, and makes its way into rivers, lakes, and aquifers. On the ground, water combines with soil and sunlight to sustain plant life. Eventually, almost all of the water evaporates back into the atmosphere.

A Thirsty Land. Demand for water is great throughout the U.S., especially where natural water resources are limited. Farmers use 140 billion gallons each day to grow crops and raise livestock. Industry needs thirty billion gallons for jobs like cooling machines and carrying waste. Individuals use up another forty billion gallons in recreation and day-to-day tasks.

People can easily use water faster than the earth can recycle it. It takes 100 years to replace water in lakes and streams. To collect water in aquifers takes as long as 5000 years. That's why it's important to save water and keep it clean.

The Earth's Water Cycle

Condensation

Rain clouds

Precipitation

Evaporation from lakes and rivers

Surface water moves rapidly in streams and eroded gullies as it moves downhill.

Lake

Evaporation from ocean

Evaporation from land

Groundwater moves slowly downhill through soil to rock without reaching aquifers.

Ocean

Lake

Aquifer

Some rain water does not soak into the ground and runs off into lakes, oceans, and rivers.

Water seeps underground from lakes and rivers into aquifers.

The earth recycles many things. Among them are the molecules of water that combine to make rivers, lakes, oceans, and aquifers. Water from the planet's surface evaporates into the clouds where it condenses around small particles of dust to form rain. Rain replaces water that has moved into the atmosphere.

Vegetation

The plants that grow in the United States have changed with human settlement. Forests that once covered most of the country have been cleared for cities and cropland. In the process, a lot of natural vegetation has been replaced by cultivated or **actual vegetation.** In Alaska and Hawaii much of the natural plant cover remains. But most of the rest of the United States is now covered with actual vegetation. This vegetation falls into several categories or zones.

Alaska

Columbia

Conifer trees such as the ponderosa pine, cedar, hemlock and Douglas fir follow the Columbia River into northern Washington and Idaho. Few broadleaf trees survive in this climate, but there is some grass for grazing cattle.

Tundra

Most of the plant cover in Alaska is natural. Alaska has a short growing season. Much of the year is cold. Most plants are low to the ground. There are some types of trees—mostly birch, aspen, alder, and spruce.

Grassland

The dry, windy climate of the central United States produces grasses with long roots that hold the soil. This zone has a variety of temperatures and growing seasons because of its size.

Pacific

Ancient forests cover a natural vegetation zone along the Northwest coast. Temperatures are mild year round. Trees include the California redwood, cedar, and Douglas fir.

Chaparral

The California chaparral has a hot, dry climate. Plants grow low to the ground. The grass cover turns brown in the winter. Broadleaf and conifer trees rarely grow higher than twenty feet here.

Mixed Forest

Mixed pine and broadleaf trees grow in areas where the natural vegetation was cleared—much of it before this century. Broadleaf trees dominate in the South while pine trees are most common along the Great Lakes.

Deciduous

Trees that lose their leaves in winter, such as oak, maple, walnut, and beech, can be found in states where there are warm summers and cold winters. Much of the vegetation here is actual.

Sierra

Following along the Sierra Nevada mountain range are needleleaf trees such as pines. High elevations and very cold, snowy winters support only a few broadleaf trees, like the oakwood.

Desert

Deserts are hot, cool, or warm. Hot areas have little vegetation. Warm and cool deserts have shrubs, grasses, and succulents like cacti.

Hawaii

Tropical

Hawaii has the most constant temperature in the United States allowing a year-round growing cycle. Seventy-five percent of Hawaii's vegetation has been introduced by humans. Natural vegetation is similar to that found in rainforests around the world.

Everglades

Magnolia, cypress, and mangrove trees grow in this area of high moisture and very warm temperatures.

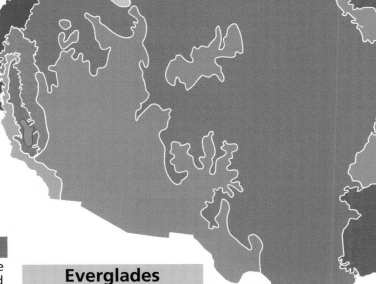

0   200   400
Miles

13

What Climate Is

You can expect it to be cool and rainy in Washington State, or hot and dry in Arizona. That's climate. **Climate** describes what the weather is like most of the time in a particular place. We describe climate by talking about how warm or cool an area is, and how much sunlight it gets. We can also describe climate in terms of precipitation—how much snowfall or rainfall a place receives.

People sometimes confuse weather with climate, but they are not the same. **Weather** occurs over a short period, while climate describes what happens over many years. The weather forecast might call for rain and cool temperatures, even in an area like Texas that has a hot, dry climate.

Several things work together in producing climates.

The Equator's Distance. Latitude, the distance a place is located from the Equator, has a major effect on the climate of a place. The closer a place is to the Equator, the more direct sunlight it receives.

Other Factors. Atmospheric pressure, the pressure of the air on the earth, also affects climate. So do wind patterns. Mountain tops have low atmospheric pressure and high winds. The climate on a mountain top usually will be drier and windier than the climate of the valley below it.

Cities	Climate Influences			Climate		
	Near Water	High Elevation	Nearer Equator	Wet	Hot Summers	Cold Winters
Albuquerque, NM			■		■	
Atlanta, GA					■	
Atlantic City, NJ	■					
Bismark, ND						■
Boise, ID		■				
Boston, MA	■					■
Charlotte, NC			■		■	
Chicago, Il	■					■
Cincinnati, OH						■
Denver, CO		■				■
Hartford, CT	■					■
Honolulu, HI	■		■	■	■	
Houston, TX	■				■	
Indianapolis, IN						■
Juneau, AK	■			■		■
Los Angeles, CA	■				■	
Memphis, TN					■	
Miami, FL	■		■	■	■	
Minneapolis, MN						■
New Orleans, LA	■			■	■	
New York, NY	■					■
Oklahoma City, OK			■		■	
Omaha, NE						■
Philadelphia, PA	■				■	■
Phoenix, AZ			■		■	
Portland, OR	■			■		
Richmond, VA	■				■	
Salt Lake City, UT		■				■
San Francisco, CA	■			■		
Seattle-Tacoma, WA	■			■		■
Trenton, NJ					■	■
Washington, DC	■				■	

14

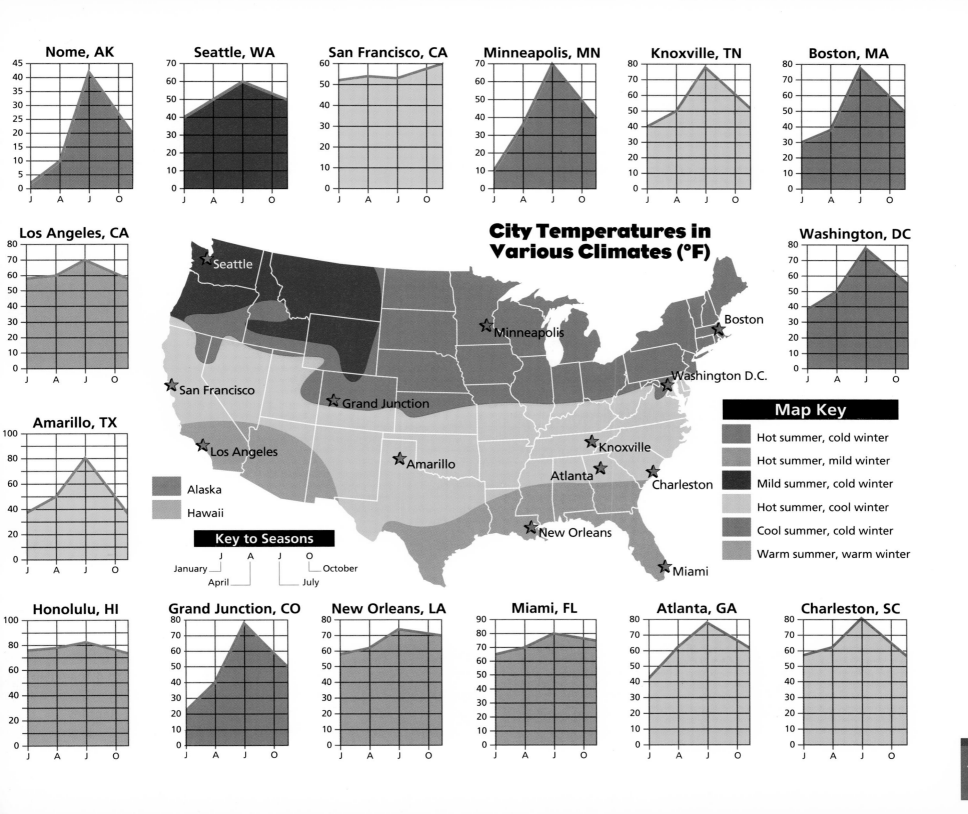

City Temperatures in Various Climates (°F)

Nome, AK

Seattle, WA

San Francisco, CA

Minneapolis, MN

Knoxville, TN

Boston, MA

Los Angeles, CA

Washington, DC

Amarillo, TX

Honolulu, HI

Grand Junction, CO

New Orleans, LA

Miami, FL

Atlanta, GA

Charleston, SC

Seattle

Minneapolis

Boston

Washington D.C.

San Francisco

Grand Junction

Los Angeles

Amarillo

Knoxville

Atlanta

Charleston

New Orleans

Miami

Alaska

Hawaii

Key to Seasons

J   A   J   O
January ⌐   ⌐   ⌐ ⌐ October
       April ⌐   ⌐ July

Map Key

Hot summer, cold winter

Hot summer, mild winter

Mild summer, cold winter

Hot summer, cool winter

Cool summer, cold winter

Warm summer, warm winter

15

How Ecosystems Work

Plants, animals, and human beings are all part of the **biosphere.** This is the region on or near the surface of the earth where living things can survive. In the biosphere, there are millions of kinds, or **species,** of plants and animals. Each species occupies a special home that scientists call a **habitat**. Plant and animal habitats often overlap. Tens, or even hundreds, of species live together in the same **biological community.**

Adaptation at Work. Living things adapt to their environments in many different ways. In deserts, cacti store water so that they have moisture during periods when it does not rain. Desert animals learn how to burrow underground to avoid the searing sun, and move about at night when it is cooler. In polar regions, seals grow thick, warm coats to protect themselves against the cold and ice. Creatures that survive in severe, cold climates store food for long winters when they cannot forage. Many hibernators sleep to conserve energy during the cold season.

Building Ecosystems. When plants and animals adapt to soil, landforms, and weather patterns by working together, they create **ecosystems**. A wide variety of soils, landforms, and climates guarantees a great range of ecosystems across our nation and around the planet.

The most important feature of these natural systems is that the creatures who share them are dependent on each other. The food chain of an ecosystem is one example of how living things are connected. Green plants may feed small animals like rabbits. Rabbits, in turn, supply food for predators, such as large birds or foxes.

Fragile. There are many elements in every ecosystem which allow the life within it to survive. When any of these elements is harmed by pollution or other changes, the ecosystem can be damaged.

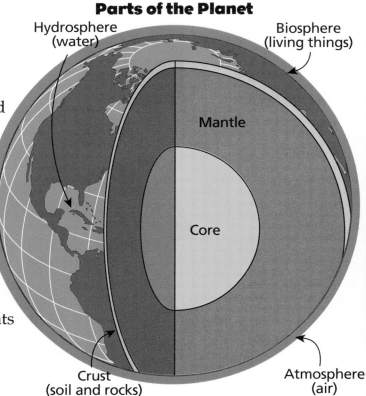

Parts of the Planet

Hydrosphere (water) · Biosphere (living things) · Mantle · Core · Crust (soil and rocks) · Atmosphere (air)

Biomes of the United States

	Example State	Average Temperature	Yearly Rainfall	Vegetation	Animals
Deciduous Forest	New York	Mild	35 inches	Deciduous	Varied
Coniferous Forest	Washington	Cool	35 inches	Needle Leaf	Varied
Grasslands	Kansas	Mild	20 inches	Grass	Varied
Mountain	Colorado	Cool	Variable	Pine	Varied
Rainforest	Hawaii	Hot	100 inches	Tropical	Varied
Cool Desert	Oregon	Cool	5 inches	Shrubs	Reptiles & Mammals
Temperate Desert	California	Mild	3 inches	Cacti	Reptiles & Mammals
Tropical Desert	Arizona	Hot	2 inches	Empty	Reptiles
Coastal	New Jersey	Mild	Variable	Variable	Varied
Tundra	Alaska	Cold	Variable	Lichen Moss	Varied
Polar	Alaska	Frigid	Variable	Empty	Mammals

Focus: The Dinosaurs' Environment

Ecosystems are fragile. Life within them depends upon the balance of many different factors. Even if one thing goes wrong in an ecosystem, a species can fail and die.

To see how this happens, we can look at the history of the dinosaur. Dinosaurs roamed the earth for 150 million years. That's more than 100 times longer than humans have lived here. Yet about sixty-three million years ago, all the dinosaurs disappeared. What happened to these strange creatures?

One Theory. Scientists have a number of explanations. But most believe something happened to the dinosaurs' environment. Evidence points to a change in climate. It's possible that the planet may have been getting colder at this time. Even the strong and resourceful dinosaur may not have been able to adapt to the cooler temperatures.

A Comet? Another theory is that the earth was struck by a giant meteorite or comet. The explosion raised huge clouds of dust and steam. These clouds were so large and heavy that they blocked the sun for many weeks. This caused the earth to get much colder. Plants and animals, including the dinosaur, were lost forever.

No one is sure which of these theories is correct. But both of them show how much living things depend upon their fragile environments.

The Dinosaur and the Comet

People

About 30,000 years ago, some people walked from what is present-day Russia into land that is now Alaska. They were the first humans to arrive in North America.

The Land Bridge. The narrow sea between Siberia and Alaska—now called the Bering Strait—was empty during an ice age that started around 35,000 B.C. People followed animals they were hunting across the land bridge. By 15,000 B.C., the sea had filled again with icy water from large, melting glaciers.

Big Game Hunters. These early people did not live in settlements. They moved constantly, hunting for huge, furry animals. These great beasts provided meat for food, and their skins were used for clothing and shelter. Eventually, these people's descendents spread throughout North, Central, and South America.

Evidence. Archaeologists have dug up many remains from these early Americans. They have found spearheads and large animal bones that show how these people hunted for and used their kill. In the modern state of Montana, they have even found the bones of prehistoric children.

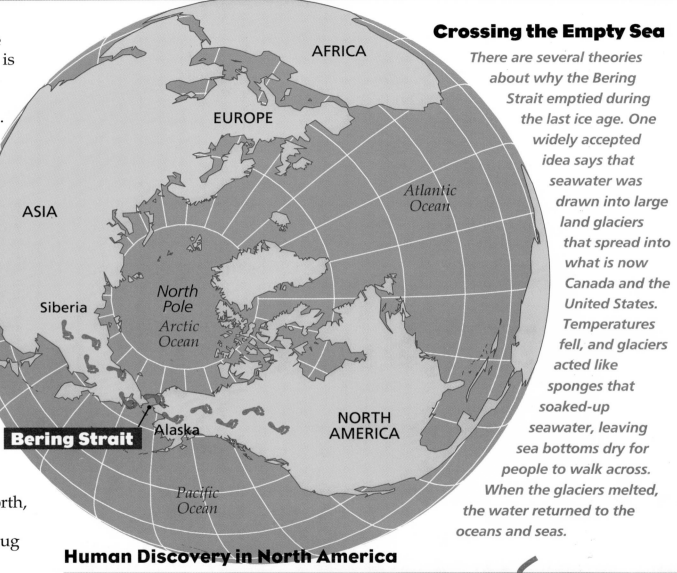

AFRICA

EUROPE

ASIA

Atlantic Ocean

Siberia

North Pole
Arctic Ocean

Bering Strait Alaska

NORTH AMERICA

Pacific Ocean

Crossing the Empty Sea

There are several theories about why the Bering Strait emptied during the last ice age. One widely accepted idea says that seawater was drawn into large land glaciers that spread into what is now Canada and the United States. Temperatures fell, and glaciers acted like sponges that soaked-up seawater, leaving sea bottoms dry for people to walk across. When the glaciers melted, the water returned to the oceans and seas.

Human Discovery in North America

First People Come to North America	Agriculture in North America Begins	Native Americans Grow Corn	Leif Ericson Arrives in Vinland
20,000	**5000**	**1000**	**1001**

B.C.   A.D.

Native Americans

The big game hunters who crossed the icy land bridge from Asia scattered throughout North America. At first they hunted **mammoths**—gigantic woolly elephants. Gradually, over 17,500 years, hunters killed mammoths, until they became extinct. For the next 6000 years, early hunters depended upon enormous herds of **bison**—early relatives of the American buffalo.

Changing Menus. By 7000 B.C., over two thousand centuries after they arrived, the earliest Americans gave up big game hunting. They began, instead, to catch small animals and fish and to gather vegetables. By this time, they knew much about the world around them and could balance their lives with the cycles of nature. In small tribes, people traveled about, hunting small animals and collecting wild vegetables from where they grew at different times of the year. This lifestyle lasted in parts of North America until about 2000 years ago.

Agriculture Begins. About the first century, tribes of Native Americans

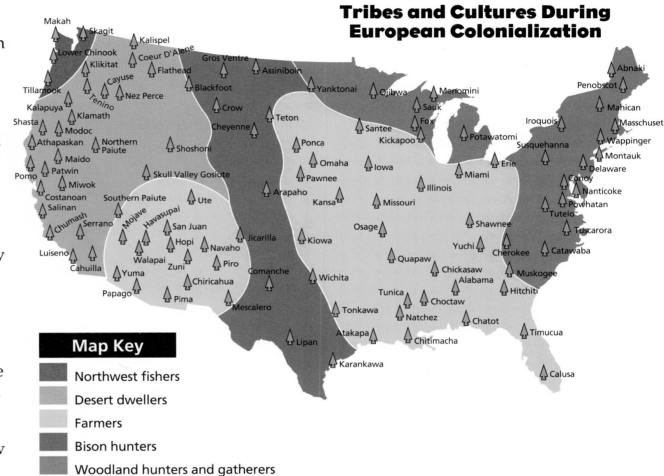

Tribes and Cultures During European Colonialization

Map Key
- Northwest fishers
- Desert dwellers
- Farmers
- Bison hunters
- Woodland hunters and gatherers

Columbus Arrives in West Indies	English Set Up Colony in Jamestown, VA
1492	1607

settled in villages and began to grow maize (corn), in rows along the ground. These villages were located in what are now the southwestern and eastern regions of the United States.

Great Civilizations. Further to the south, in what is now Mexico and Central and South America, complex civilizations grew out of early Native American settlements. Temples, pyramids, palaces, and cities were built in places that Europeans would name Peru and Mexico.

These civilizations, like the lifestyles of the Native Americans in the United States, would be destroyed when Europeans arrived in the fifteenth and sixteenth centuries.

The Europeans Arrive

The rich spice markets of Asia attracted seafarers in the 1400s. Europeans in search of easy trade routes set sail in merchant ships. One of their most important "discoveries" was North America, a continent that covers nearly a quarter of the earth's surface. Soon explorers realized their accidental luck. The newfound continent was not Asia, but it was filled with many valuable resources.

Part of the Treasury. Since feudal times, kings and queens had owned most of Europe's land. They parceled it out to the warriors who fought for them, or gave holdings to other valued subjects. When new lands were discovered across the ocean, these European monarchs expected to own them as well. They did not recognize the rights of those people who had lived in these territories for hundreds of thousands of years.

To European conquerors, "civilization" meant consuming everything nature had to offer. Because Native Americans farmed with simple tools, Europeans thought they did not know how to "use" the land. Europeans concluded that all the resources of the Americas were rightfully theirs. For three centuries, England, France, Spain, and other European governments sent colonists to strip treasures from the Americas. Their cultures' values would replace the Native American practice of living in balance with the environment.

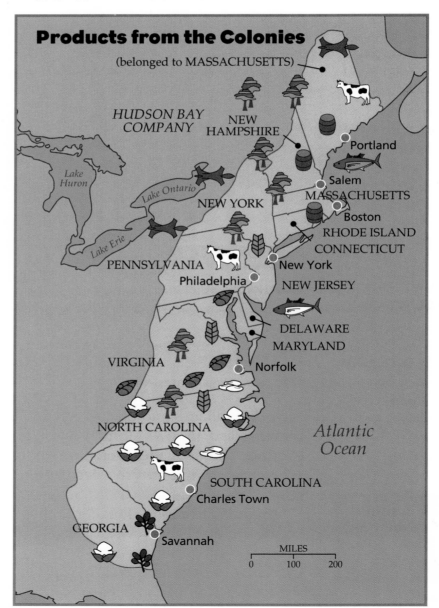

Products from the Colonies

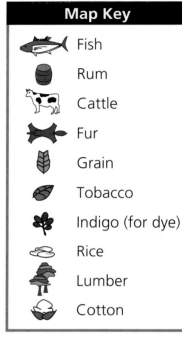

Map Key

Fish	
Rum	
Cattle	
Fur	
Grain	
Tobacco	
Indigo (for dye)	
Rice	
Lumber	
Cotton	

In the American colonies, the English were able to find or grow products, such as fur and grain, that they needed back home. They also introduced American products, such as tobacco, to Europe. Colonists were allowed to cut and use the wood of ancient forests for shipbuilding, heating, and home construction, but they were not encouraged to manufacture goods.

Settling the Seaboard. Early European settlers stayed close to the Atlantic Coast. By the sixteenth century, many English settlements dotted the seaboard. As the coast grew crowded, settlers crept westward into the tree-covered frontier.

The English idea of settling land was to create open space by cutting forests, and using the wood for building and for fuel. Settlers also cleared acre upon acre to grow their own food and raise agricultural products that were shipped to Europe. These raw materials, like flax and wool, were turned into manufactured goods in Europe and returned to the colonies for sale.

Lost Habitats. Eventually, some colonists shipped lumber and livestock to the West Indies in return for slaves imported from Africa. Using slaves, the Europeans cleared even more land for rice and cotton plantations. In doing this, settlers destroyed many plant and animal habitats. They also destroyed the habitats of Native American peoples who used the natural vegetation to supply food, shelter, and medicine. These peoples had no immunity to the diseases Europeans brought over, and epidemics of diseases like smallpox killed many of them. Environmental stress and wars with settlers pushed a number of tribes to extinction.

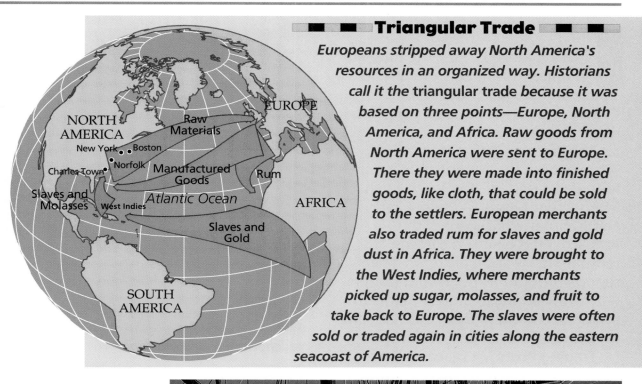

■ ■ Triangular Trade ■ ■ ■

Europeans stripped away North America's resources in an organized way. Historians call it the triangular trade *because it was based on three points—Europe, North America, and Africa. Raw goods from North America were sent to Europe. There they were made into finished goods, like cloth, that could be sold to the settlers. European merchants also traded rum for slaves and gold dust in Africa. They were brought to the West Indies, where merchants picked up sugar, molasses, and fruit to take back to Europe. The slaves were often sold or traded again in cities along the eastern seacoast of America.*

*Near the Statue of Liberty there is an exact copy of Henry Hudson's ship the Half Moon. **The ship is wonderfully colored, exactly the way it was in 1609.***

Conflict on the Frontier

In less than 200 years, the English colonies expanded from 891,000 square miles to an independent United States that covered over three times as much land in 1848.

The Frontier Trail. European settlement of the American frontier followed a pattern. Explorers such as Meriwether Lewis, William Clark, and Zebulon Pike scouted the undiscovered country, earning reputations as "trail blazers". Their reports brought trappers and traders who retraced the explorers' paths in search of resources that could be sold in cities in the East and in Europe.

Trading Posts. At places where trails met or rivers connected, traders and pioneers built trading posts and forts to exchange goods. The forts also provided protection from the people they incorrectly called Indians. As the wilderness was explored, settlers followed the trappers and buffalo hunters. They built sod houses, and eventually cabins, across the great prairies.

Defeat. Native Americans living on the Great Plains fought against the destruction of their habitats. Battles with U.S. troops raged through the nineteenth century. In December of 1890, at Wounded Knee in South Dakota, U.S. soldiers killed nearly 300 Sioux, including many women and children. Afterwards, there was no serious resistance to white settlement.

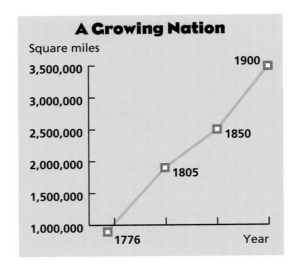

A Growing Nation

Square miles

3,500,000 — 1900
3,000,000
2,500,000 — 1850
2,000,000 — 1805
1,500,000
1,000,000 — 1776   Year

Pioneers traveled in covered wagons which they abandoned when they reached their destinations.

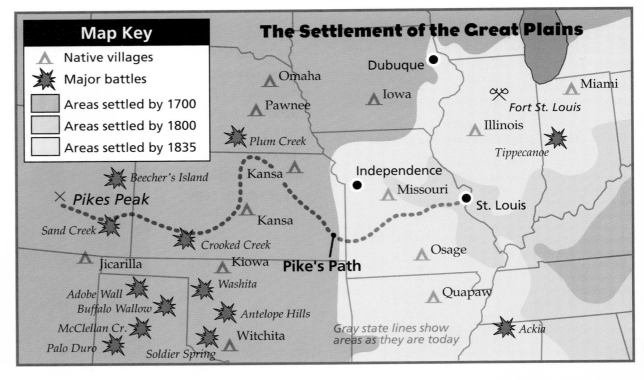

The Settlement of the Great Plains

Map Key

⚠ Native villages
✴ Major battles
▨ Areas settled by 1700
▨ Areas settled by 1800
▨ Areas settled by 1835

Omaha
Dubuque
Iowa
Miami
Pawnee
Fort St. Louis
Illinois
Plum Creek
Tippecanoe
Beecher's Island
Kansa
Independence
✕ Pikes Peak
Missouri
St. Louis
Sand Creek
Kansa
Crooked Creek
Pike's Path
Osage
Jicarilla
Kiowa
Washita
Quapaw
Adobe Wall
Buffalo Wallow
Antelope Hills
McClellan Cr.
Ackia
Palo Duro
Witchita
Gray state lines show areas as they are today
Soldier Spring

Focus: Colonial Environmental Problems

The destruction of Native American habitats in North America was the major environmental disaster of colonial times. But few colonists realized it. They were, however, aware of other environmental problems. Most occurred in towns and cities that were carved roughly out of the wilderness.

Ancient Problems. We think of urban environmental issues as something new. But they are as old as cities themselves. When people crowd together, garbage and waste are always issues. Keeping streets and water supplies safe and clean is a major job. In ancient times, the Romans built **aqueducts** to carry fresh water into the city because local rivers were too polluted to drink.

In eighteenth century Philadelphia, Ben Franklin had clean water to drink and fresh food to eat. But he awoke each day to the overpowering stench of rotting animal carcasses. An assortment of leather tanyards and meat-rendering plants stood only yards away from his doorstep.

Creek Disappears. The 1770 map of Franklin's neighborhood near Independence Hall shows Dock Creek. In Franklin's time, it was filled in with silt, animal remains, and other wastes. Eventually the creek disappeared. You cannot find it in modern Philadelphia.

Today, zoning and anti-pollution laws require industries to build far away from residential areas. And they must dispose of waste properly.

Polluting Franklin's Neighborhood in Colonial Philadelphia

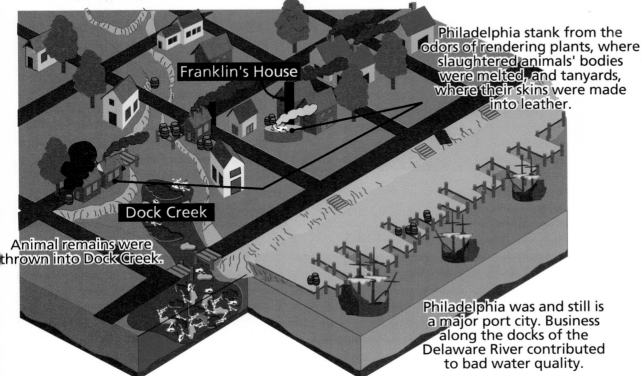

Franklin's House

Dock Creek

Animal remains were thrown into Dock Creek.

Philadelphia stank from the odors of rendering plants, where slaughtered animals' bodies were melted, and tanyards, where their skins were made into leather.

Philadelphia was and still is a major port city. Business along the docks of the Delaware River contributed to bad water quality.

Visitors come to Independence Hall by the thousands each year. The monument stands for the principals of our democracy. The area is now part of the National Park system, and is kept much better than it was in Franklin's time.

Forests

Most of the ancient forests that once covered the United States gradually were cut down. Even so, almost one-third of the United States is still covered by forests. Much of this tree cover has been planted in the past 400 years.

Forests provide protected environments for many species of plants and wildlife. They provide people with places to hike, picnic, hunt, or camp. They provide wood for manufacturing, giving jobs to millions of Americans. For the planet as a whole, forests make life—the air we breathe, the climate that nurtures us—possible.

Endangered. Today forests are in danger. Each year many acres of tree cover are cleared for agriculture and commercial development. In parts of the country, especially the Northwest, timber companies fight to harvest trees, and environmentalists oppose them. Trees as old as 3000 years are being cut.

Tree Hazards. Forests also must survive increased pollution. Acid rain kills or stunts some trees. In New England, acid rain may have caused a drop in maple syrup production. High ozone levels (from car pollution) disturb photosynthesis, causing trees to lose leaves and needles. Other air pollutants leave trees weak, and easy targets for disease, insects, and drought.

Forests protect the soil from erosion. They absorb carbon dioxide and turn it into oxygen that animals and people need to breathe. Forests also clean pollution from the air and help keep the earth's climate cool. This forest in Oregon was growing when Europeans first came to North America.

Growth of a Forest

Annual weeds Perennial weeds and grasses Shrubs Young pine forest Developed deciduous forest

0   3   5   25   75   175

Years

1620

Ancient Forests

When European colonists first came to America, the forests were so thick that in some places a person could not walk through them. Today only six percent of those ancient forests are standing. Most can be found in the Pacific Northwest. They include magnificent giant redwoods and sequoias. Some of the oldest trees in the world, 4000-year-old bristlecone pines, grow in California. Ancient, or old-growth forests *are important because they are complete biological communities. In them many different species interact and depend on each other for survival. A good word for this is* biodiversity. *It means that many things live and work together. Forests planted by humans have less biodiversity.*

Today

DID YOU KNOW ?

- In the United States, 71.8% of all forests are owned by U.S. citizens and the remaining forests are owned by the government.

- Pine forests become more common as you travel away from the Equator.

- Tall mountains have timberlines above which trees will not grow.

- Forests cover 34% of the earth.

- Tree leaves and needles have a waxy coating that protects them from water loss and insects. Pollution can eat that coating away and leave trees unprotected.

Map Key

 Ancient forests
(does not show
new-growth forests)

Using Wood

Forests shape our lives. Each of us uses many paper and wood products every day. Three quarters of a million people in the United States work as loggers, in saw mills, as shapers of wood, in plywood construction, and building wood containers. Businesses also export millions of feet of lumber to other countries, such as Japan.

Many states, such as Oregon, Washington, and California, rely on taxes from lumber companies to help pay for highways, schools, and other public needs.

Cutting Forests. With the high value placed on wood products, many of America's forests are being cut to the ground. Even when wood is not cut for wood products, forests are being cleared for mining, agriculture, and ranching. Trees are downed to make way for dams and man-made lakes that will provide electricity.

Using National Forests. Not even the National Forests are safe from exploitation. In 1990, eleven billion feet of lumber were cut from the National Forest system by companies that bought leases from the federal government. Thousands of acres in other areas were rented to private companies to graze livestock and to build roads, bridges, and railroads.

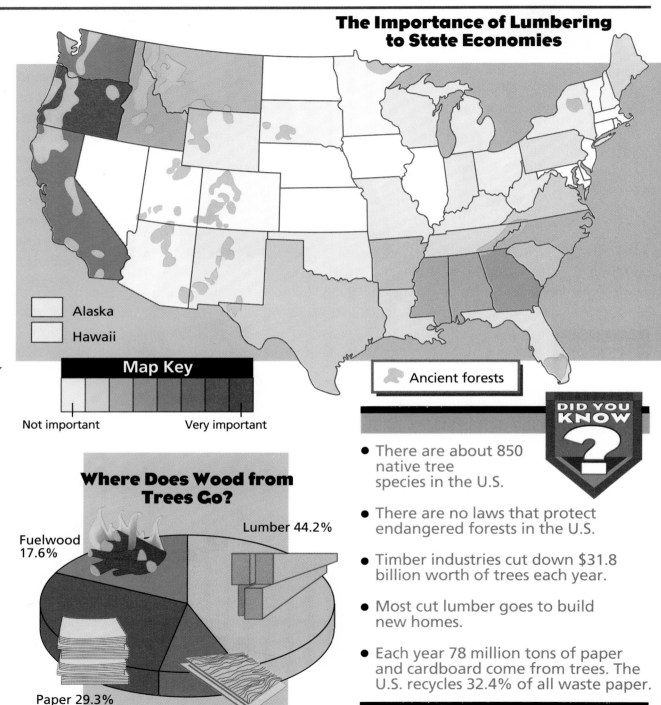

The Importance of Lumbering to State Economies

Alaska

Hawaii

Map Key

Not important   Very important

Ancient forests

Where Does Wood from Trees Go?

Fuelwood 17.6%

Lumber 44.2%

Paper 29.3%

Plywood 8.9%

DID YOU KNOW?

- There are about 850 native tree species in the U.S.

- There are no laws that protect endangered forests in the U.S.

- Timber industries cut down $31.8 billion worth of trees each year.

- Most cut lumber goes to build new homes.

- Each year 78 million tons of paper and cardboard come from trees. The U.S. recycles 32.4% of all waste paper.

Caring for Our Forests

When European colonists first came to America, the forests were so thick in spots that a person could not walk through them. Today, ninety-percent of that original tree cover is gone. The demands to cut the last six percent increase every day.

Clearly, we should think before we cut our forests. A single species of tree can provide habitats for 300 other species of plants and animals. Trees also clean our air, stop erosion, and keep the climate from overheating.

Useful products. Our forests need protection, but we also need to use them. Lumber companies supply important materials such as wood, syrups, dyes, seeds, resins, and even medicines. They also provide jobs to millions of people. Our challenge is to conserve and protect forests as we use them.

Saving for the Future. Recycling materials like paper, cardboard, and packaging material can reduce the number of trees we use. In many areas, people are learning to cut selectively instead of clear-cutting forests, which destroys the entire habitat. Scientists are developing tree seedlings that mature faster. These trees can be grown like crops to serve many of our pulp and wood needs. The farming of forests is called **silviculture.**

Many communities have tree planting projects in which every citizen can participate. In recent years, families are also buying live holiday trees and planting them when the holiday season has ended. What these children are doing in our photograph will have a lasting effect. Their activities will bring beauty to their neighborhoods and good health to everyone's environment.

Clear-cutting is very destructive to forests and wildlife habitats. Better lumbering methods take fewer trees from each area.

Save a forest by...

- using fewer paper products and recycling the ones you use.

- carpooling to reduce air pollution that threatens trees.

- asking your governmental representatives to oppose logging in National Forests.

- buying paper products made from recycled materials.

- using a cloth sack instead of paper (or plastic).

- following park rules about setting fires in camping areas.

Preserving National Forests and Parks

The spectacular waterfalls of Yosemite, the sculpted curve of the Grand Canyon, the exotic wildlife of the Everglades—all these are part of our National Park system. The range and splendor of these natural wonders are unequaled anywhere else on earth. In recent years more and more Americans have taken notice of this great national resource.

Overuse. The very popularity of national forests and parks has become something of a problem. Each year 300 million people visit national parks alone. Millions more visit state and local parks. The sheer number of tourists has put strains on the park system. The steady traffic is starting to destroy the very habitats— and species—that people have come to see. Damage to the environment, crowding, litter, and animal interference are all problems that need to be faced.

Solutions. In order for plants, animals, and humans to continue to enjoy these dramatic environments, changes must be made. In some parks, areas are blocked off during parts of the year. This gives animals privacy in seasons when mating and giving birth take place. In other parks, cars have been banned. They may be replaced by nonpolluting, open-air trams that move people from one site to another. These efforts will help keep our parks a treasure for future centuries.

Yosemite National Park in California is one of the nation's most beautiful places. It is also one of its most crowded. This trail to Vernal Falls is beaten down by a steady flow of eager hikers.

Swift Current Lake and Mount Wilbur in Montana's Glacier National Park are treasures that all Americans hope will last for generations.

Focus: Jobs vs. an Endangered Species

The northern spotted owl may be America's most famous endangered species. It lives in Douglas fir trees in the Pacific Northwest. These trees are at least 200 years old.

Owls and Their Space. Like many birds that prey on small animals that live on the forest floor, the spotted owl needs a large area in which to look for food. An average pair of owls might hunt for mice, squirrels, and other animals in a space as large as 4500 acres.

In 1990, there were only about 1700 pairs of these birds left alive in the United States. The Fish and Wildlife Service added the northern spotted owl to its endangered species list. A three-million-acre piece of Pacific forest was set aside for the owls' habitat.

Opposing Arguments. Lumber companies now think the President and Congress should overrule the decision to protect the owls. They want to cut timber in the ancient forest that is the owl's main habitat. They argue that jobs for people are much more important than a single type of bird.

On the other side of the battle are environmental groups, who claim that the owl is only a small part of a much larger issue. Many species might be lost if we keep cutting our forests. We may even lose some plants and animals that we haven't yet discovered.

Why Do Species Become Endangered?

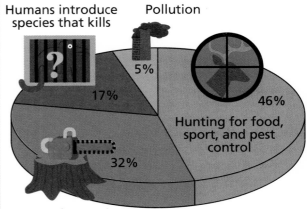

- Humans introduce species that kills — 17%
- Pollution — 5%
- Hunting for food, sport, and pest control — 46%
- Habitat destruction, such as logging and wetland draining — 32%

DID YOU KNOW?

- In the U.S. alone, there are more than 100 endangered species.

- Animals in other countries, like the thick-billed parrot, become endangered when people capture them for sale in the U.S.

- More than 300 wildlife refuges in the U.S. protect threatened animals.

- The endangered Devil's Hole pupfish lives only in a small pool in the middle of the Nevada desert.

- California Condors are so threatened that researchers are trying to breed them in captivity.

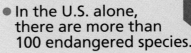

Spotted Owl Habitat

Farms

The United States is blessed with moderate temperatures, good rainfall, and some of the world's richest soils. It is not surprising that our nation grows plenty of food for its own people and exports farm products to other nations.

Many Farms, Many Crops. Farming means different things in different parts of the country. Across the United States, crops change with soil and climate variations. In New Jersey, where nights are warmed by gentle breezes from the Atlantic Ocean, farms grow fruits and vegetables that are shipped to stores and end up on dinner tables in nearby cities. In South Carolina, farmers grow tobacco on small plots of land in a humid climate.

In California, thousands of acres of fertile soil are moistened by irrigation. Great quantities of fruits and vegetables grow on large, corporate farms. These crops are sent to markets throughout the United States and to foreign countries.

Livestock. Farms also raise livestock for meat and dairy products. In dry parts of the country, ranchers raise cattle that feed on a rich diet of prairie grasses. In mountainous areas, farmers raise sheep and goats. In the fertile states in the Midwest, farmers grow corn to feed dairy cows.

Different crops need different irrigation methods. Sometimes water is pumped into shallow valleys between rows. Other methods, like this one, spin water in giant circles above thirsty plants, much like a rotating lawn sprinkler.

DID YOU KNOW?

- The average family of four spends about $130 a week on food.

- Most family farmers own about 580 acres.

- On average, the largest farms are in Arizona and the smallest are in Rhode Island.

- About 13% of U.S. farmland is irrigated.

- In 1820, 70% of people were farmers; in 1992, less than 2% were.

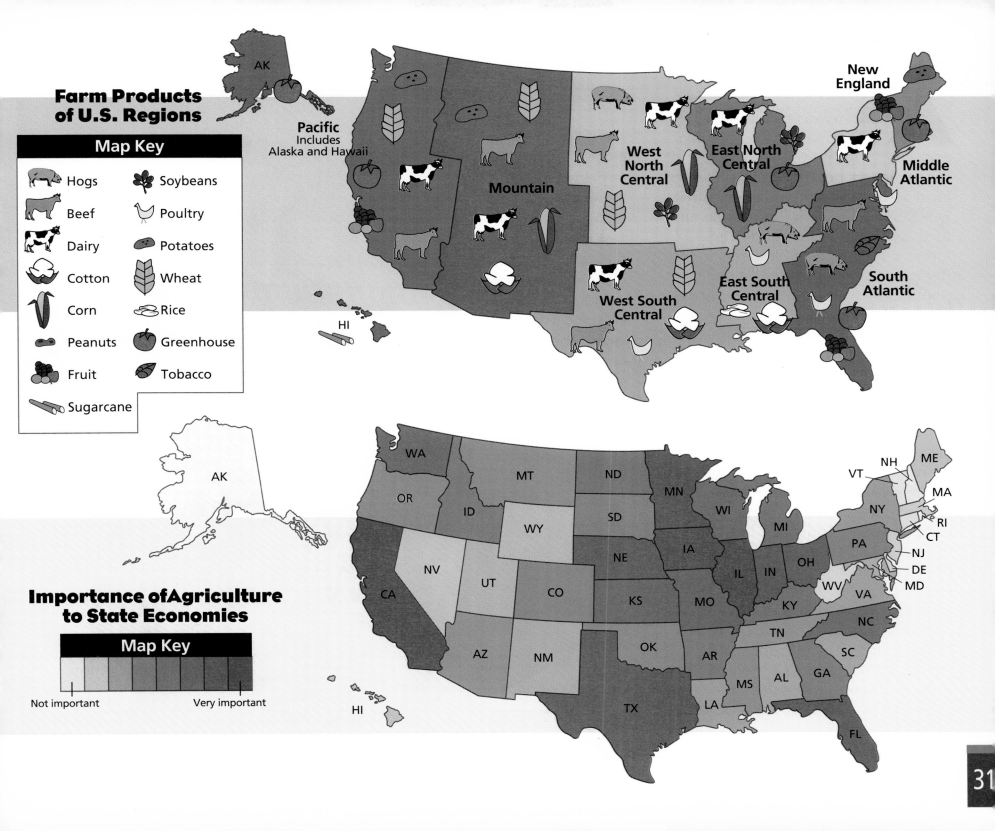

Farm Products of U.S. Regions

Map Key

- Hogs
- Beef
- Dairy
- Cotton
- Corn
- Peanuts
- Fruit
- Sugarcane
- Soybeans
- Poultry
- Potatoes
- Wheat
- Rice
- Greenhouse
- Tobacco

Pacific
Includes Alaska and Hawaii

Mountain

West North Central

East North Central

New England

Middle Atlantic

West South Central

East South Central

South Atlantic

Importance of Agriculture to State Economies

Map Key

Not important — Very important

The Growing American Farm

American farms are growing, but people are leaving them every day. This may seem like a contradiction, but it's not. The average farm is sixty-six percent larger than it was thirty years ago. At the same time, there are fewer farms and fewer farmers. Just twenty years ago, almost five percent of the United States' population lived on farms. Today, less than two percent do.

Giving Up. Many family farmers have lost their land because they cannot afford to pay the debt on it any longer. Others have given up farming because they can't make a profit. Today, every state government has a program to help preserve family farms and to keep them in business.

Family Farms vs. Big Business. Farming, like so many things in our competitive economy, has become serious business. Corporations have combined small farms to make large farm businesses. New corporate farms use modern equipment and are, in some ways, more efficient. But they also use large amounts of limited resources, like water. They employ fewer workers per acre than family farms. Many people question whether or not corporations will have as much interest in taking care of the land as family farmers.

Agriculture is a modern industry. Farmers rarely work the land with simple tools. This automated feed plant in Kansas turns grain into an easily digested, highly nutritious food for livestock. With such equipment, farmers can manage larger farms and herds.

Average Farm Size

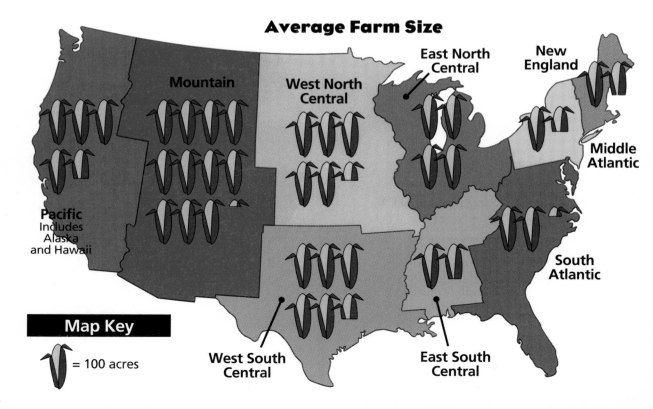

East North Central

New England

Mountain

West North Central

Middle Atlantic

Pacific
Includes Alaska and Hawaii

South Atlantic

Map Key

= 100 acres

West South Central

East South Central

Farms and Water Supplies

Many of the most fertile areas in the United States have little rain. All of California, our most productive farm state, falls into this category.

Irrigation. When soil is rich and water is scarce, farmers irrigate land to grow crops. In 1960, thirty-three million acres of farmland were irrigated. In 1990, that number increased to 250 million acres. Irrigation sometimes takes water away from aquifers faster than it can be replaced by rainfall.

Fertilizers. Other areas of the United States have poor soil and plentiful rain. Here farmers use fertilizers to make soil more productive.

Chemical fertilizers, along with pesticides and herbicides, create larger harvests for farmers. But they also can cause serious environmental damage.

Water Pollution. Sometimes farm chemicals are washed into slow-moving rivers and lakes. When this happens, plant life in these waters grows out of control, choking out fish and other animals.

Fertilizers and pesticides can also soak into the ground. These chemicals seep through the soil into aquifers, making the water unsafe for drinking. In 1990, the EPA found pesticides in the groundwater of twenty-six different states. If those waters are

tapped again for irrigation, even more chemicals are added, damaging supplies even further.

Healthy Farms. Farmers and government officials are looking for ways to keep chemicals out of the water supply. Some growers have turned to organic farming. This type of farming uses natural methods to keep crops healthy such as friendly insects that consume harmful pests. Other farmers are resorting to "dry farming" methods which use considerably less water. Many states now have programs to counsel individual farmers. With help they can make their farms profitable and healthy.

Irrigation

States needing no irrigation because they have good rainfall

Map Key

Slight   Moderate   Intense

The government is reducing farm pollution by...

- making laws that stop farmers and gardeners from using fertilizers and insecticides that are dangerous to people and animals.

- educating farmers about what they can do to help the environment.

- making free maps for farmers that show them where endangered species live so that farmers can avoid areas where animals make their homes.

- giving tax breaks to farmers who are willing to leave some of their land unused.

Erosion

Soil erosion is often found in areas that have been cleared for farming. Once plants and their roots have been removed, wind and water can carry the soil away. How much erosion takes place depends upon how hard the winds are blowing and how rapidly the water moves.

Effects of Wind and Water. Wind erosion usually takes place gradually, and its effects are hard to detect. We can look at the ground, however, to see how water changes the land. Sometimes it clears soil from broad areas. This is called **sheet erosion.** Other times, it moves quickly down hill, carving channels in a process called **gully erosion.**

Plant Protection. The only protection that an ecosystem has against erosion is vegetation. Plants slow down erosion by blocking wind and slowing the movement of water. Their roots provide a structure to which the soil can cling.

Farming, construction, logging, mining, and other human activities often leave the ground vulnerable to wind and water erosion by removing too much vegetation. One way farmers can reduce erosion is by rotating crops from one field to another rather than plant the same crop on the same land each year.

Erosion shapes landscapes in a dramatic fashion. Sometimes wind moves soil away from the earth over a long period of time. In other cases, water cuts quickly into the soil and whole sections of hillsides collapse.

Wind and Water Erosion

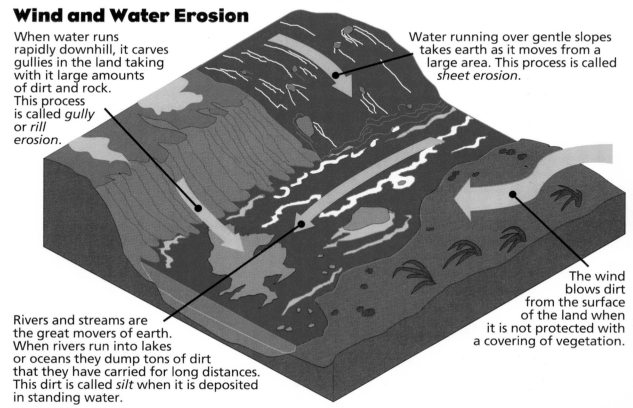

When water runs rapidly downhill, it carves gullies in the land taking with it large amounts of dirt and rock. This process is called *gully* or *rill* erosion.

Water running over gentle slopes takes earth as it moves from a large area. This process is called *sheet erosion.*

Rivers and streams are the great movers of earth. When rivers run into lakes or oceans they dump tons of dirt that they have carried for long distances. This dirt is called *silt* when it is deposited in standing water.

The wind blows dirt from the surface of the land when it is not protected with a covering of vegetation.

Focus: Erosion Crisis, The Dust Bowl

In 1930, America had one of its worst environmental disasters. A large fertile area on the prairies of the southern Great Plains lost its topsoil cover. It came to be known as the Dust Bowl. The "bowl" covered large parts of Kansas, Texas, and Oklahoma, and extended into Arizona and New Mexico.

Grass Destroyed. The Great Plains are hot and dry. In many years, rainfall is good, but in other years it doesn't meet the needs of farmers. The Great Plains are also windy. But natural grasses that once covered the prairies had deep root systems that held the soil to the ground during droughts and high winds.

Farmers, however, didn't realize the value of grass in the prairie ecosystem. When they first came to the land, they plowed the grass away and planted crops with short root systems, such as corn. In some years, they left parts of land unplanted and unprotected.

Soil in the Wind. When the hot prairie winds blew across the plowed plains, the shallow roots of farm crops could not hold the soil in place. Millions and millions of tons of topsoil blew into the sky. This created a cloud that blocked out the sun for miles around. The topsoil eventually blew as far as 1500 miles from its original location, dusting the entire East Coast of the United States.

When the drought ended, a farming area the size of Connecticut and Maryland was destroyed. Thousands of farmers went bankrupt, and most were forced to move to other states to find new land and jobs.

Remedies. The crisis did have one positive effect. In 1935, Congress passed the Soil Conservation Act. Soil conservation districts were set up all over the nation to give farmers advice on using the land wisely. Today many anti-erosion practices are used on American farms. And they are working. Since 1985, farmers have cut topsoil erosion by a third.

Dust Bowl of the Southwest

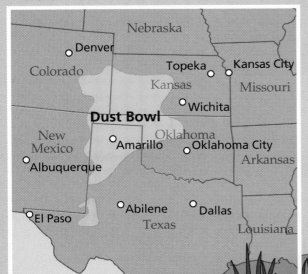

What Happens When Grass is Plowed

- Vegetation protects soil. It shades it from the sun. It stops harsh winds. Its roots provide a network of strands that soil holds on to. When people remove vegetation, they also remove nature's protection from erosion.

- Unprotected soil dries into a fine powder. When wind and water pass over unprotected soil, it erodes much faster. The soil of the Dust Bowl eroded quickly because people removed protective prairie grasses.

Wind lifts dry unprotected soil from the plains of Southwestern states.

Unprotected soil

Cities like New York, Boston, and Philadelphia are homes to millions of people today. But they also played big parts in the colonial economy. All were located on bays or rivers. All had ports that received goods from the American agricultural heartland and shipped them across the sea to Europe.

From Trade to Manufacturing. After the American Revolution, investors in the United States were able to begin manufacturing here. They built factories near shipping ports. They created roads and canals to carry products to and from the American countryside.

The Industrial Revolution changed American cities once more, as residents turned their attention from trade to manufacturing. More people found work in the city and began to live there, some in the shadow of smokestacks that supplied their livelihood. Industrialization made the U.S. more prosperous, while it also polluted many cities. Widespread use of the automobile in the twentieth century made the air even dirtier.

Move to the Suburbs. After World War II, many city dwellers moved to newly-built suburbs in search of clean air and open countryside. Workers

Behind the industrial skylines of early American cities were a generation of workers who put in long hours running huge machines. Laborers worked as many as eighteen hours a day and six or seven days a week in dirty factories.

commuted from suburb to city by automobile, bus, or train.

The Service Economy. By the 1960s, the economy of the United States had begun to change from manufacturing industries to service and lighter industries. Factories were replaced by office buildings, and fewer people lived downtown. Workers moved further into the suburbs, and business sometimes followed. Families purchased millions of cars to take them from home to work, and from

shopping center to shopping center.

Today, most people live in metropolitan areas. The borders of major cities often stretch into each other. Baltimore, Maryland, and Washington, DC, for example, form one huge suburban city that covers many miles. These suburban cities are connected by highway systems that create even greater air pollution. Some cities, like Los Angeles, must alter their fragile natural environments to support millions of people.

Today, more people work in offices than one hundred years ago. They may commute to work many miles each day.

The automobile has changed the way that Americans live. It has allowed them to expand the area in which they can work, shop, and play. One hundred years ago, people shopped in stores in their own neighborhoods. Today, many people shop in malls that are miles away. The automobile has also created air pollution, noise, and congestion. Reducing car use is one of the best ways to improve our environment.

Challenges and Solutions for Modern Cities

C: Reduce congestion and overcrowding.

S: Build and take care of parks. Develop bicycle, walking, and jogging paths.

C: Reduce air pollution from automobiles.

S: Use mass transit like subways and buses. Car-pool. Make commuter lanes on highways for cars with more than one passenger.

C: Reduce noise pollution caused by cars, airplanes, trucks, and factories.

S: Outlaw horn honking. Build sound barriers near highways. Move noisy factories away from where people live.

C: Reduce solid waste.

S: Expand recycling facilities; reduce litter.

C: Solve parking problems.

S: Walk, ride bikes, car-pool or use mass transit when going to work.

C: Reduce litter.

S: Build community pride. Educate people about their roles and responsibilities in their communities.

37

Where People Live

hy is population an environmental issue? Because many environmental problems are caused by large numbers of people competing for space and resources. More people create more trash. More people consume more things made by industries that pollute the water and air. More people drive more cars, which congest cities and produce more smog. More people use more natural resources, such as water, soil, and energy. As population grows, natural resources are used faster than the earth's systems can replace them.

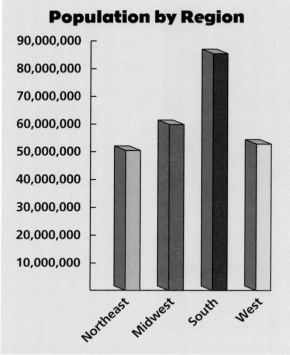

Population by Region

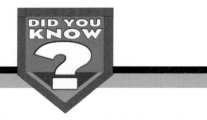

- As of 1990, there were 248,709,873 people in the United States.

- There are 15.9 births each year for every 1000 people.

- The average age of people in the United States is 32.8.

- There are 95 males for every 100 females.

- There are 18,354,000 children under 5 years old.

- More than three quarters of the U.S. population lives in metropolitan areas.

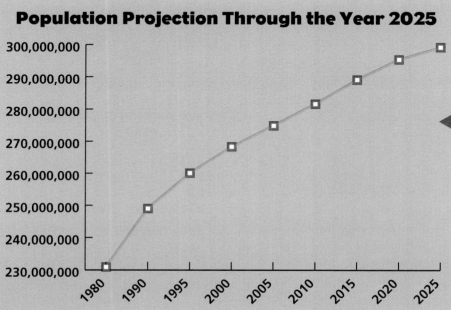

Population Projection Through the Year 2025

Population grows when more people are born than die. In the United States, about 15 children are born for every 8.7 who die. Between 1981 and 1990, immigrants accounted for almost one-third of U.S. population growth.

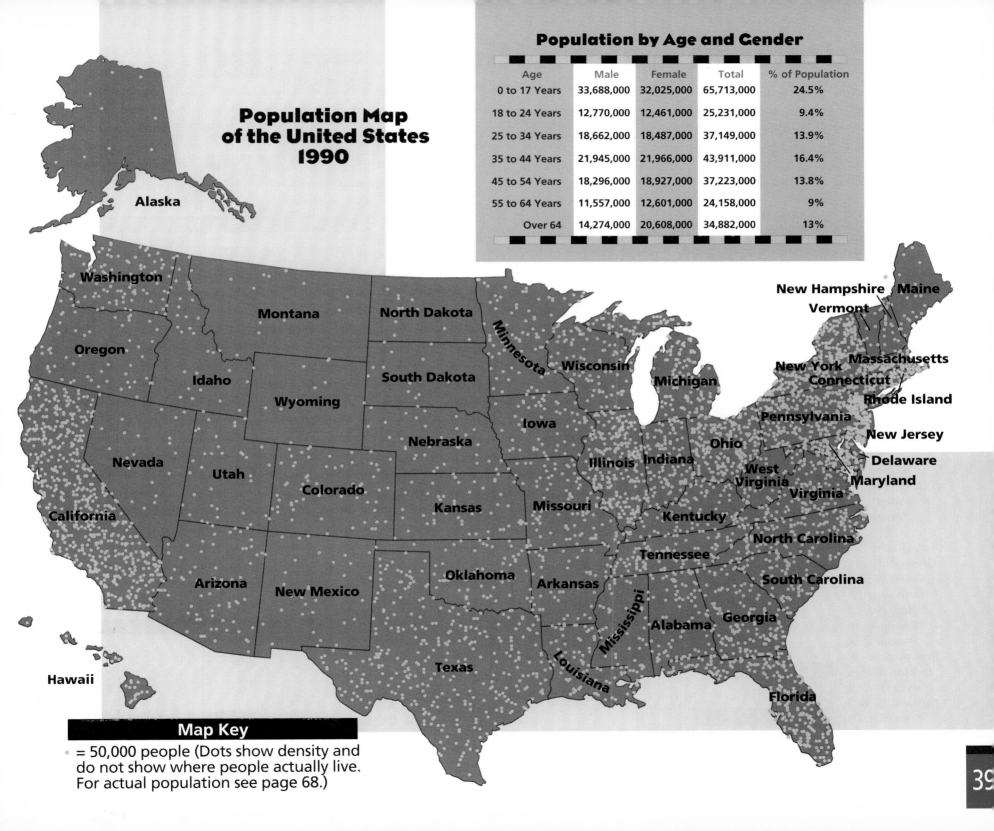

Population Map of the United States 1990

Population by Age and Gender

Age	Male	Female	Total	% of Population
0 to 17 Years	33,688,000	32,025,000	65,713,000	24.5%
18 to 24 Years	12,770,000	12,461,000	25,231,000	9.4%
25 to 34 Years	18,662,000	18,487,000	37,149,000	13.9%
35 to 44 Years	21,945,000	21,966,000	43,911,000	16.4%
45 to 54 Years	18,296,000	18,927,000	37,223,000	13.8%
55 to 64 Years	11,557,000	12,601,000	24,158,000	9%
Over 64	14,274,000	20,608,000	34,882,000	13%

Alaska

Washington
Oregon
Montana
North Dakota
Minnesota
Wisconsin
Michigan
New Hampshire
Maine
Vermont
New York
Massachusetts
Connecticut
Rhode Island
Pennsylvania
New Jersey
Idaho
South Dakota
Iowa
Ohio
Delaware
Wyoming
Nebraska
Illinois
Indiana
West Virginia
Maryland
Nevada
Utah
Colorado
Kansas
Missouri
Kentucky
Virginia
California
North Carolina
Tennessee
Arizona
New Mexico
Oklahoma
Arkansas
Mississippi
South Carolina
Georgia
Alabama
Texas
Louisiana
Florida
Hawaii

Map Key

= 50,000 people (Dots show density and do not show where people actually live. For actual population see page 68.)

Air Quality in Major Cities

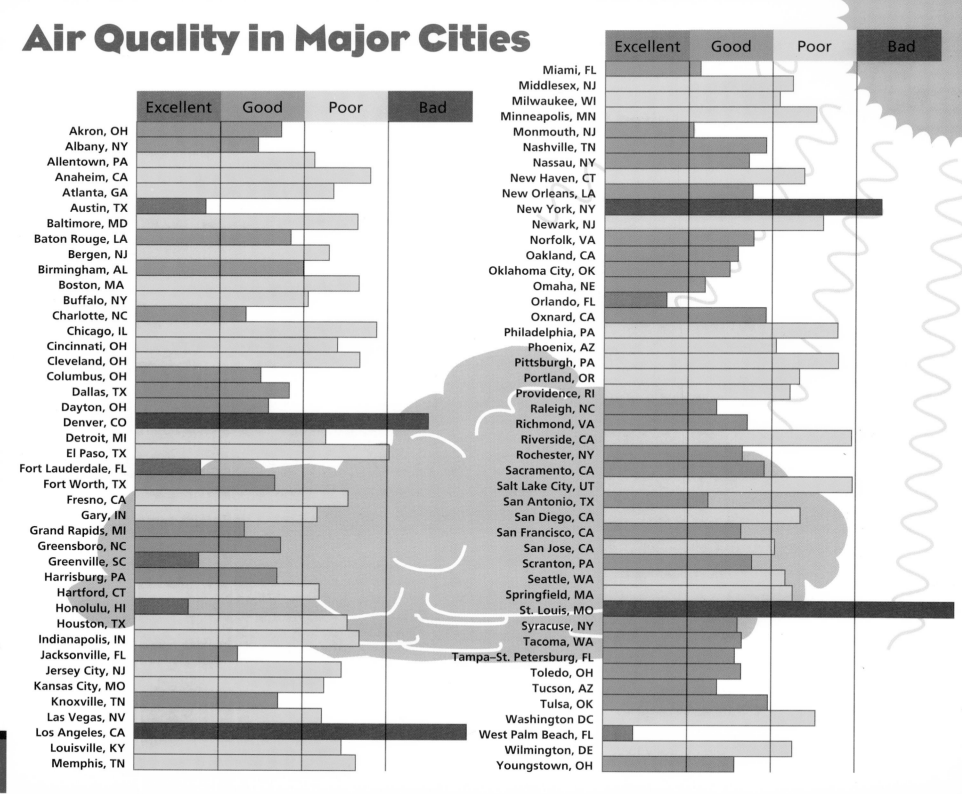

	Excellent	Good	Poor	Bad
Akron, OH				
Albany, NY				
Allentown, PA				
Anaheim, CA				
Atlanta, GA				
Austin, TX				
Baltimore, MD				
Baton Rouge, LA				
Bergen, NJ				
Birmingham, AL				
Boston, MA				
Buffalo, NY				
Charlotte, NC				
Chicago, IL				
Cincinnati, OH				
Cleveland, OH				
Columbus, OH				
Dallas, TX				
Dayton, OH				
Denver, CO				
Detroit, MI				
El Paso, TX				
Fort Lauderdale, FL				
Fort Worth, TX				
Fresno, CA				
Gary, IN				
Grand Rapids, MI				
Greensboro, NC				
Greenville, SC				
Harrisburg, PA				
Hartford, CT				
Honolulu, HI				
Houston, TX				
Indianapolis, IN				
Jacksonville, FL				
Jersey City, NJ				
Kansas City, MO				
Knoxville, TN				
Las Vegas, NV				
Los Angeles, CA				
Louisville, KY				
Memphis, TN				

	Excellent	Good	Poor	Bad
Miami, FL				
Middlesex, NJ				
Milwaukee, WI				
Minneapolis, MN				
Monmouth, NJ				
Nashville, TN				
Nassau, NY				
New Haven, CT				
New Orleans, LA				
New York, NY				
Newark, NJ				
Norfolk, VA				
Oakland, CA				
Oklahoma City, OK				
Omaha, NE				
Orlando, FL				
Oxnard, CA				
Philadelphia, PA				
Phoenix, AZ				
Pittsburgh, PA				
Portland, OR				
Providence, RI				
Raleigh, NC				
Richmond, VA				
Riverside, CA				
Rochester, NY				
Sacramento, CA				
Salt Lake City, UT				
San Antonio, TX				
San Diego, CA				
San Francisco, CA				
San Jose, CA				
Scranton, PA				
Seattle, WA				
Springfield, MA				
St. Louis, MO				
Syracuse, NY				
Tacoma, WA				
Tampa–St. Petersburg, FL				
Toledo, OH				
Tucson, AZ				
Tulsa, OK				
Washington DC				
West Palm Beach, FL				
Wilmington, DE				
Youngstown, OH				

Focus: How Pittsburgh Cleaned Up

Pittsburgh became an industrial, steel-making giant about 100 years ago. Three major rivers—the Monongahela, the Ohio, and the Allegheny—meet in this western Pennsylvania city. These rivers were used to move iron ore and coal into Pittsburgh's furnaces, and to move finished steel out.

Eventually, the rivers became polluted and started flooding. Belching smokestacks dirtied the air. Huge heaps of slag, the waste from making steel, blemished the earth.

First Clean-up. In the 1950s, industrialists and political leaders joined together to clean up the city. They passed anti-smoke laws to clean up the air. They created locks and dams to tame the rivers. They replaced industrial slums with parks, plazas, and modern buildings.

By the 1970s, Pittsburgh's steel factories were outdated, and the steel industry was failing. As jobs were lost, neighborhoods crumbled.

Good Place to Live. City leaders again joined together to bring in clean industries that use technologies such as biomedicine, robotics, and software to create new jobs. In 1985, Pittsburgh was named America's most livable city. Today, people can even fish in the Monongahela.

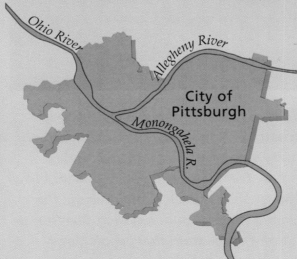

Pittsburgh's Three Rivers

Ohio River

Allegheny River

City of Pittsburgh

Monongahela R.

Pittsburgh

Here is what Pittsburgh looked like when its steel mills were thriving, and how it looks today. Industry in the cities around the Great Lakes—especially steel-works—had declined so much by the 1980s that the area was often described as the Rust Belt.

Bottles and cans are solid wastes. So are scraps from manufacturing and ash from smokestacks. Most **solid waste**—trash that isn't liquid or gas—comes from industry and manufacturing.

Only one and one-half percent comes from families and businesses. Its technical name is **municipal waste,** but we usually call it garbage. About 185 million tons of garbage are produced each year. Each person throws away an average of about 1400 pounds of the stuff. It would take a line of garbage trucks 150,000 miles long to carry all the municipal waste made in a year in the United States.

Where to Put It. As of 1990, twenty-seven states were having problems finding space to dump trash. Some states have started to send trash to other states and even to other countries. In 1987, a boat-load of trash sailed from New York to South America for dumping. It was met by foreign gunboats that turned it around. The trash was finally burned in Brooklyn, New York, but only after six months of debate.

The Landfill Issue. Landfills provide a ready dumping ground for non-hazardous waste, but these spaces are running out. And some landfills create their own hazards. Older ones have no lining and wastes can filter down through soil and into the water supply. In most landfills little air is available to decompose the waste. Items buried 20 years ago have been dug up completely intact.

Trash is heavy. Each bag weighs about twenty-eight pounds. Each person throws away a stack of bags each year that is fifteen feet high—and getting higher. To control solid wastes, many towns in the United States require recycling. Sixty-three percent of the trash that people throw away can be recycled.

Industrial Waste. More than ninety-eight percent of waste comes from mining, natural gas production, industry, and agriculture. Industry has become somewhat efficient in recycling scrap metal and paper because, in large quantities, they are quite valuable. Progress has also been made in creating smokestacks that filter out particles of ash that escape incineration. Much work needs to be done to dispose safely of waste material that results from mining and of sludge that often contains chemicals.

DID YOU KNOW?

- Hot dogs last more than ten years in a landfill.

- It costs Americans $6 billion a year to take their trash away. That's about $100 for a family of four.

- Some states charge a fee for soda bottles. They give the money back when a customer returns the bottles for recycling.

- Methane, a gas created from decomposing waste in landfills, can sometimes be tapped as a source of energy.

- Several businesses in the U.S. now rescue throwaways from landfills and dumps and sell them for profit.

We can reduce trash problems by recycling. We can also ask our government to ban throwaway items, like plastic bottles. Tax breaks could be used to reward companies who put their products in recyclable containers.

How Much Trash Do We Make Each Year?

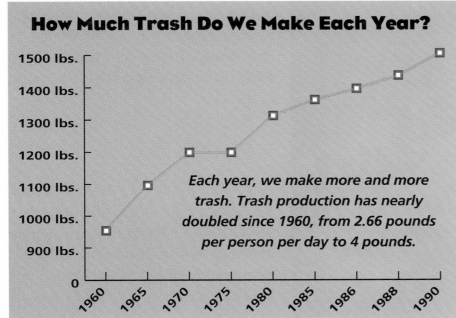

Each year, we make more and more trash. Trash production has nearly doubled since 1960, from 2.66 pounds per person per day to 4 pounds.

What Do We Throw Out As Solid Waste?

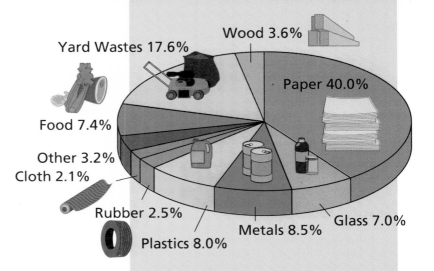

Wood 3.6%
Yard Wastes 17.6%
Paper 40.0%
Food 7.4%
Other 3.2%
Cloth 2.1%
Rubber 2.5%
Metals 8.5%
Glass 7.0%
Plastics 8.0%

Waste Pollution

Waste disposal generally falls into two categories—throwaway and low-waste. Throwaway methods include **incineration**, or burning, and landfilling. These are the most common ways to dispose of solid waste in the United States. Low-waste methods include recycling and composting. These practices are newer and are gaining popularity.

Thoughtless Throwaways. Until twenty years ago, people didn't think much about air pollution caused by incineration. They were not concerned about burying millions of tons of garbage under the earth. They didn't know yet that landfills give off gases that contribute to global warming and pollute underground water supplies. People didn't realize that the world's valuable, unrenewable resources were being wasted when aluminum cans and copper pipes were thrown away.

Low-waste Increases. As concerns about discarding valuable materials grows, and space for landfills runs out, support for low-waste methods is growing. More manufacturers are turning to recycled materials for making their products.

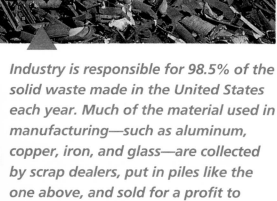

Industry is responsible for 98.5% of the solid waste made in the United States each year. Much of the material used in manufacturing—such as aluminum, copper, iron, and glass—are collected by scrap dealers, put in piles like the one above, and sold for a profit to other manufacturing businesses.

Where Does Our Trash Go?

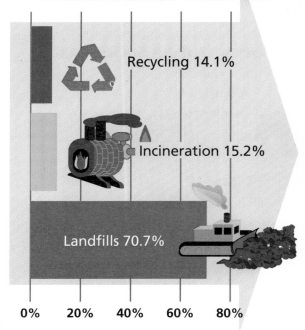

Recycling 14.1%

Incineration 15.2%

Landfills 70.7%

0%   20%   40%   60%   80%

People put trash where they think no one will see it. This trash heap is typical of dumps that are hidden just behind trees in some of our nation's most beautiful places.

Recycling: Learning from Nature

Nature recycles everything that it creates. Water moves from the ground into the sky, and comes back down to earth in different places at different times. Even death means new life. Plants and animals die in the forest and enrich the soil for future generations of life.

New Ways. People are learning to be more like nature in handling waste. In the U.S., we are moving away from dumping, burying, and burning, and moving towards recycling, reusing, and reducing waste.

A few years ago people began to collect paper, bottles, cans, and plastics to be broken down and made into new products. Many are starting to understand that recycling helps conserve our limited natural resources. It also puts less pressure on overfull landfills.

Kids' Work. In most families, kids are the biggest recyclers. They have made it their responsibiltiy to carry recycled materials to their front yards or to recycling centers. In many towns, schools are recycling collection points.

Recycling seems to be working. Today recycling of aluminum cans has reached sixty-two percent. Nearly a third of all glass containers and eleven percent of plastic bottles and containers are recycled.

Recycling Laws

Map Key
States with recycling laws

There are no recycling laws in Alaska or Hawaii.

What Percent of Waste Made Each Year is Recycled

Paper	25.6%
Iron/steel	5.8%
Aluminum	31.7%
Other metals	65.1%
Glass	12%
Plastics	1.1%
Yard wastes	1.6%
Other	2.1%

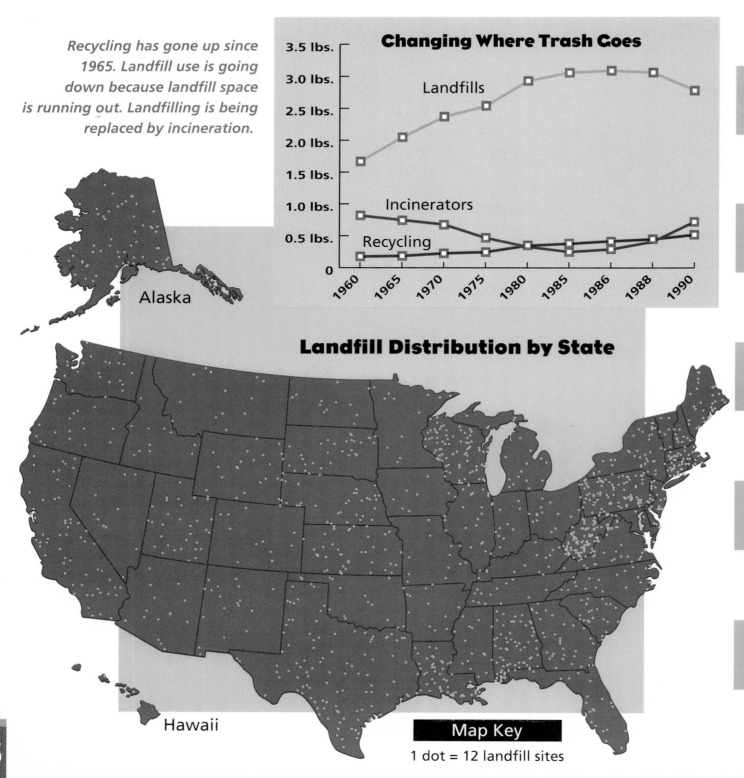

Recycling has gone up since 1965. Landfill use is going down because landfill space is running out. Landfilling is being replaced by incineration.

Changing Where Trash Goes

Landfills

Incinerators

Recycling

3.5 lbs.
3.0 lbs.
2.5 lbs.
2.0 lbs.
1.5 lbs.
1.0 lbs.
0.5 lbs.
0

1960 1965 1970 1975 1980 1985 1986 1988 1990

Landfill Distribution by State

Alaska

Hawaii

Map Key

1 dot = 12 landfill sites

Landfills

States that are running out of space for landfills are red

Alabama	800
Alaska	740
Arizona	185
Arkansas	116
California	720
Colorado	130
Connecticut	188
Delaware	37
Florida	238
Georgia	390
Hawaii	25
Idaho	126
Illinois	275
Indiana	131
Iowa	102
Kansas	463
Kentucky	181
Louisiana	618
Maine	362
Maryland	16
Massachusetts	249
Michigan	257
Minnesota	160
Mississippi	195
Missouri	138
Montana	170
Nebraska	413
Nevada	117
New Hampshire	125
New Jersey	108
New Mexico	214
New York	522
North Carolina	243
North Dakota	139
Ohio	211
Oklahoma	173
Oregon	220
Pennsylvania	1204
Rhode Island	13
South Carolina	286
South Dakota	357
Tennessee	166
Texas	1201
Utah	375
Vermont	101
Virginia	264
Washington	260
West Virginia	1209
Wisconsin	1033
Wyoming	300

Taking Care of Dangerous Wastes

Hundreds of the chemicals that we use in the United States can be harmful to humans and animals. Many are used by industry to manufacture products. Others, such as paint and automobile oil, are used by individuals. Disposing of these dangerous waste products is a problem.

Often, when people are finished with toxic materials, they dump them in the ground, release them into the air, or pour them into lakes and rivers. In 1989 alone, 300 billion pounds of poisonous waste were disposed of in the United States. That is about fifty pounds for every citizen.

Love Canal. In too many cases, toxic wastes have been dumped where they can hurt people and wildlife. The New York community of Love Canal was abandoned in 1978, when people discovered that they were living directly on top of 22,000 tons of toxic, cancer-producing wastes. A chemical company had put poisons into drums that were buried several feet below the ground, and covered with dirt. Most of the drums were buried under the school playground. Children began to come home with skin burns. More people started dying from cancer. Finally, city and state officials were forced by concerned citizens to recognize the problem.

Taking Care. Some powerful and

toxic chemicals are important to our survival. If businesses or individuals use toxic chemicals, they should also be responsible for cleaning them up. Better methods of disposing of toxic wastes are being developed, and new laws have been written to require people to use them.

Hidden toxic wastes are ticking time bombs. People may not discover their location until someone gets sick. Most dump sites are listed, however, and laws have been passed to force some of the dumpers to clean up these areas.

The Many Problems with Toxic Wastes

Well

Aquifer

1. Fish—and those that eat them—can become poisoned by chemicals that seep from polluted aquifers into lakes and streams.

2. Fruit and vegetable-producing plants take in toxins through their roots.

3. Farms, homes, and businesses dig wells that can tap into polluted aquifers.

4. Barrels of toxic wastes are dangerous. When the barrels get old and leaky, chemicals soak down to aquifers or rise to the land's surface. Although they may be invisible, chemicals can make people sick or burn their skin.

5. When animals eat grass that has roots in contaminated soil, it can poison them.

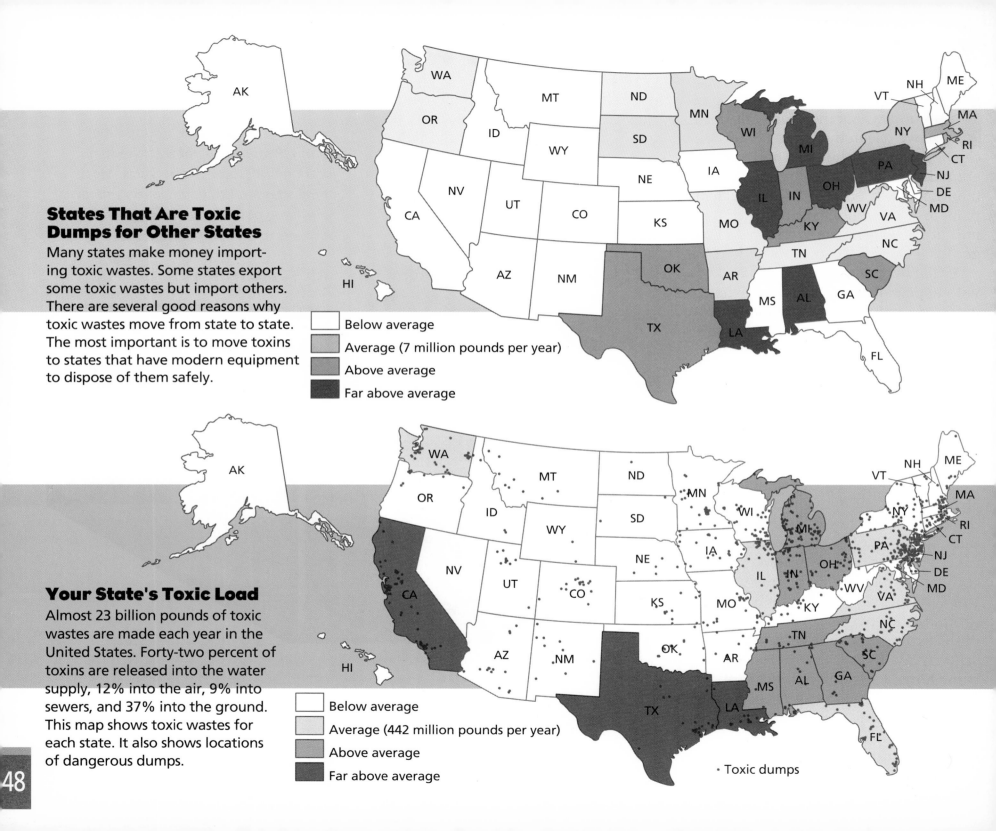

States That Are Toxic Dumps for Other States

Many states make money importing toxic wastes. Some states export some toxic wastes but import others. There are several good reasons why toxic wastes move from state to state. The most important is to move toxins to states that have modern equipment to dispose of them safely.

Below average

Average (7 million pounds per year)

Above average

Far above average

Your State's Toxic Load

Almost 23 billion pounds of toxic wastes are made each year in the United States. Forty-two percent of toxins are released into the water supply, 12% into the air, 9% into sewers, and 37% into the ground. This map shows toxic wastes for each state. It also shows locations of dangerous dumps.

Below average

Average (442 million pounds per year)

Above average

Far above average

• Toxic dumps

Focus: Making Steam from Trash

Not everyone agrees on how to solve environmental problems. One waste disposal method about which people strongly disagree is trash-to-steam incineration. Some people believe that burning trash is a good way to make energy to run electrical generators. People who oppose this method say that the amount of electricity produced is small, compared to the amount of pollution that incineration makes.

A New Kind of Burning. Many communities have burned trash for years to keep landfills open and to kill bacteria that live in solid waste. Trash-to-steam incineration is a little different. It uses the heat that comes from burning trash to boil water. The steam from this water is then used to power generators that produce electricity. The electricity is either sold or used to provide power to burn more trash in the incinerator itself.

People who favor trash-to-steam say that sixty percent of all trash can be burned with good incinerators. They say that this process prevents adding to landfills. They also say that trash-to-steam incinerators create jobs and save electricity.

The Opposition. On the other side, people point out that trash-to-steam incineration puts toxic gases and tons of hazardous ash into the atmosphere. They also have shown that paper recycling saves five times as much energy as trash-to-steam incineration makes.

Currently, there are 128 trash-to-steam incinerators in the United States. Sixty-four proposed new incinerator projects have been blocked by environmentalists and members of the communities where they are to be built. As with many environmental issues, the answers to problems of waste disposal are not simple.

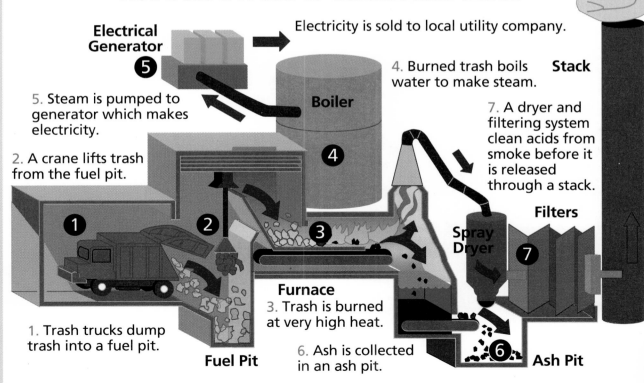

How Does a Trash-to-Steam Plant Work?

Electricity is sold to local utility company.

Electrical Generator

5. Steam is pumped to generator which makes electricity.

2. A crane lifts trash from the fuel pit.

Boiler

4. Burned trash boils water to make steam.

7. A dryer and filtering system clean acids from smoke before it is released through a stack.

Stack

Filters

Spray Dryer

Furnace

3. Trash is burned at very high heat.

1. Trash trucks dump trash into a fuel pit.

Fuel Pit

6. Ash is collected in an ash pit.

Ash Pit

Air Resources

The earth's atmosphere is a blanket of gases that reaches 300 miles into the sky. It contains traces of many elements, but it is mostly a combination of oxygen, nitrogen, and argon. Gravity holds the atmosphere close to the earth. The higher we go into the atmosphere, the more gas molecules spread out. The amount of air on a mountain top is less than that at ground level.

Life in the Troposphere. Four layers make up the earth's atmosphere—the troposphere, the stratosphere, the mesosphere, and the thermosphere. The troposphere is the part of the atmosphere that affects weather and climate. Most of the water vapor and dust in the earth's atmosphere is here. The troposphere's water vapor condenses and falls to the ground as rain or snow. This layer of the atmosphere is in constant motion. Air currents move clouds and water vapor around the planet every minute of every day.

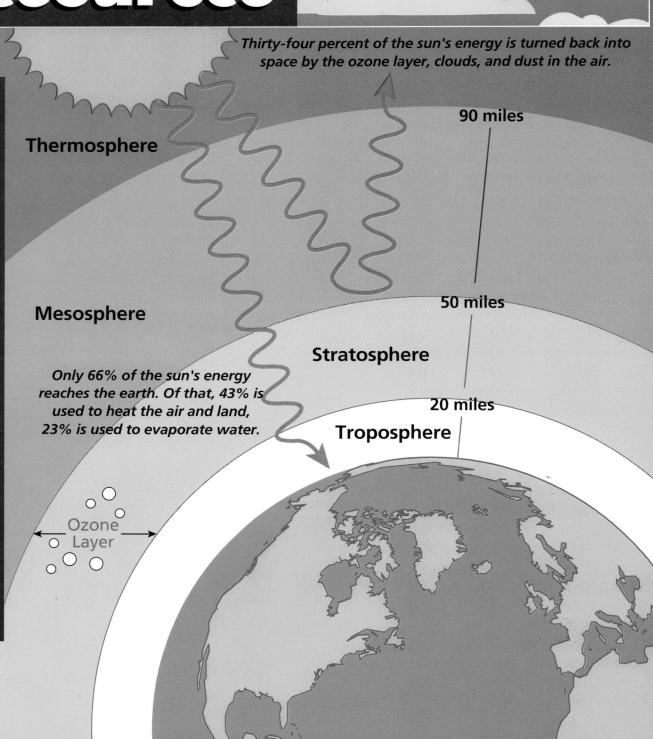

Thirty-four percent of the sun's energy is turned back into space by the ozone layer, clouds, and dust in the air.

Thermosphere

90 miles

Mesosphere

50 miles

Stratosphere

Only 66% of the sun's energy reaches the earth. Of that, 43% is used to heat the air and land, 23% is used to evaporate water.

20 miles

Troposphere

Ozone Layer

Sources of Air Pollution

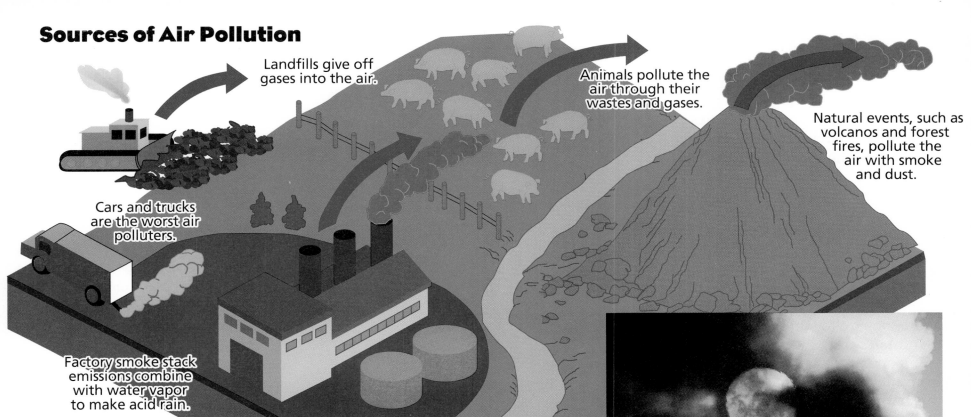

Landfills give off gases into the air.

Animals pollute the air through their wastes and gases.

Natural events, such as volcanos and forest fires, pollute the air with smoke and dust.

Cars and trucks are the worst air polluters.

Factory smoke stack emissions combine with water vapor to make acid rain.

How Much Pollution Comes from Each Source?

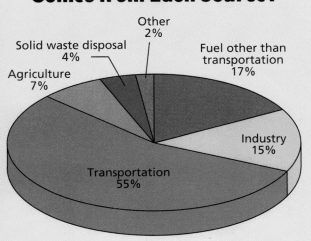

Other 2%

Solid waste disposal 4%

Agriculture 7%

Fuel other than transportation 17%

Industry 15%

Transportation 55%

Many factories burn coal for energy in their manufacturing processes. Smokestack emissions contribute to air pollution because they contain sulfur—a chemical that causes breathing problems. Sulfur combines with water in the air to produce acid rain. In recent years, industries have learned how to reduce this kind of pollution. They are beginning to use cleaner fuels and can filter pollutants from the smoke at the top of the stack.

The Ozone Layer

In the upper stratosphere, about twelve miles above the earth's surface, is a thin layer of gas called ozone. This transparent gas helps protect life on the earth, and it is increasingly in danger.

Protection From Radiation. Life on our planet depends on the sun's energy. But some parts of the sun's radiation are harmful—particularly ultraviolet waves. Anyone who has been badly sunburned knows that overexposure to sunlight is dangerous to human skin.

Ozone protects people and plants from ultraviolet light. It stops much of this harmful radiation before it gets to the earth's surface. Each one percent loss of ozone in the upper stratosphere results in a seven percent increase in skin cancer.

Damage to the ozone layer also causes other human health problems, such as eye cataracts, and lung problems from increased smog production.

Damaging Chemicals. Some of the chemicals that humans use—like the chloroflourocarbons (CFCs) in refrigerators and air-conditioners— harm the ozone layer as they rise in the atmosphere. In order to prevent more damage, the United States, Japan, and Russia have agreed to reduce CFC use 100 percent by the year 2000.

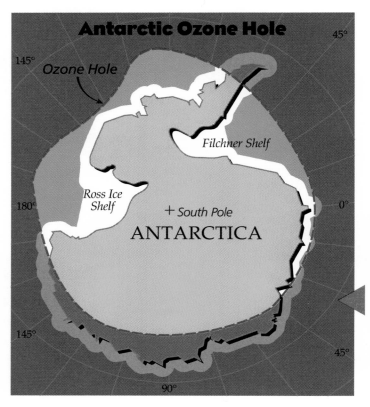

Antarctic Ozone Hole

145°
Ozone Hole
45°
Filchner Shelf
Ross Ice Shelf
180°
+ South Pole
ANTARCTICA
0°
145°
45°
90°

Scientists measure ozone in the earth's stratosphere using satellites. The ozone layer is getting thinner in most places. Over some parts of the planet, like Antarctica, the layer is completely gone. Without the protection of ozone, the sun's harmful rays threaten all living things. While few people live in Antarctica, other holes are growing over populated areas like New England.

How Can We Protect the Ozone Layer?

- Keep refrigerators and freezers closed as much as possible.

- Keep air-conditioners clean and running efficiently. Where possible, use fans instead of air-conditioning.

- Don't purchase foam products. When burned or left in landfills, they can damage the ozone layer.

- Use recyclable paper or plastic cups instead of ozone-damaging Styrofoam.

The Greenhouse Effect

1. Sunlight travels 93 million miles to warm the earth. Sunlight reflects off the earth's surface and goes back to space.

2. Greenhouse gases—carbon dioxide, water vapor, ozone, methane, nitrous oxide, and chlorofluorocarbons—in the earth's upper atmosphere trap some of the heat that is reflected from the earth's surface.

3. People add greenhouse gases to the atmosphere when they live and work on the earth. This causes more heat to be trapped and the earth's climate to get warmer.

Thirty thousand years ago, half of North America was covered with ice. Yet, the average temperature of the earth was just nine degrees Fahrenheit colder than it is today. Life, as we know it now, was made possible by a few degrees of warming in the earth's climate.

Balanced for Life. Over the last 10,000 years, the temperature has reached a productive balance. It is warm enough for plants to grow in many regions of the planet. It is cool enough so that the water they need does not evaporate too rapidly. Any change in this balance would make life on Earth much more limited.

The Greenhouse Effect. The earth's temperature is partly controlled by the atmosphere. Heat from the ground rises and is trapped by gases in the troposphere and the stratosphere. This sequence of events resembles what happens in a greenhouse. Trapped heat warms the planet and keeps it from turning into an iceberg. But if too much heat becomes trapped in the atmosphere, the earth's climate could get very hot.

Getting Hotter. Scientists believe that the earth is actually getting warmer. The year 1990 was the warmest in this century. Six of the warmest years in the twentieth century occurred during the 1980s. This trend in climate is called **global warming**. The rise in temperature may be being caused by human activities, like burning fossil fuels for energy.

The clear-cutting of tropical forests could be adding to the problem. Vast areas of trees and plants are being burnt to clear land. The burning releases carbon dioxide into the atmosphere. At the same time the earth is losing the plants it needs to absorb this gas and convert it into oxygen.

What We Could Lose. Some scientists believe that world temperatures might rise as much as nine degrees. An increase of nine degrees would reshape the earth's biomes. Wetlands would become dry, and some farming areas would get too hot to grow crops.

There is even a theory that a temperature increase of less than two degrees would melt the polar icecaps. Melting the icecaps would create a twenty foot rise in mean sea level around the world. As the seas rose, coastal cities would be flooded. As much as one-fifth of the world's people would be homeless.

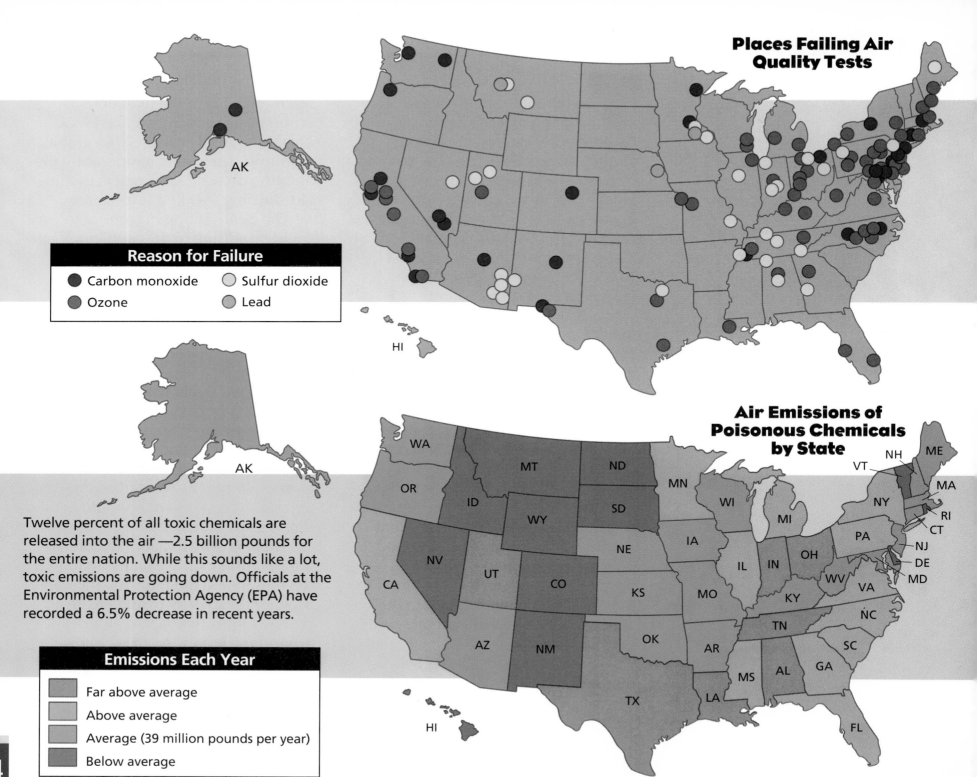

Places Failing Air Quality Tests

Reason for Failure
- ● Carbon monoxide
- ○ Sulfur dioxide
- ● Ozone
- ● Lead

AK

HI

Air Emissions of Poisonous Chemicals by State

Twelve percent of all toxic chemicals are released into the air —2.5 billion pounds for the entire nation. While this sounds like a lot, toxic emissions are going down. Officials at the Environmental Protection Agency (EPA) have recorded a 6.5% decrease in recent years.

AK

Emissions Each Year
- Far above average
- Above average
- Average (39 million pounds per year)
- Below average

WA, OR, ID, MT, ND, MN, WI, MI, NY, VT, NH, ME, MA, RI, CT, NJ, DE, MD, PA, OH, WV, VA, NC, SC, GA, KY, TN, AL, MS, LA, AR, OK, KS, MO, IL, IN, NE, IA, WY, CO, UT, NV, CA, AZ, NM, TX, HI, FL

54

FOCUS: Smog Alert in Donora

Smog is a compound that is made when polluted air is heated. Cities with the worst smog usually have warm, dry climates, large populations, and many cars. There is little precipitation to rinse smog particles from the air.

Smog becomes especially dangerous when it is trapped above a city and is not blown away by the wind. Los Angeles, Denver, Salt Lake City, and Donora, Pennsylvania are all located in valleys with wind circulation problems. All have problems with gray or brown smog.

Deadly Air. In 1948, many of Donora, Pennsylvania's 14,000 citizens started to complain about headaches, dizziness, vomiting, and diarrhea. Twenty of them became so sick they died. The U.S. Public Health Service investigated the situation and found that Donora's air was being poisoned by a large amount of chemicals.

Warnings. Donora's problem helped people focus on industrial pollution and its effect on public health. Today, most communities issue warnings when smog levels are high. Older people and all those with respiratory problems are instructed to stay indoors.

There are two types of smog. One turns the sky gray. It comes from burned coal particles that mix with water in the air. The other colors the sky brown. It comes from a heated mixture of gasoline fumes and air in warm, dry cities, like Los Angeles.

Thermal Inversion in Donora

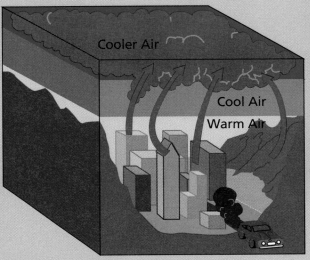

Normal Condition

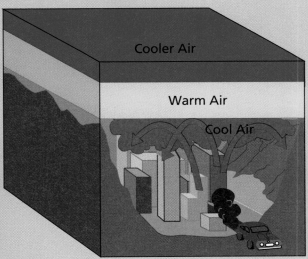

Thermal Inversion

Normally, warm air rises into the cool upper atmosphere carrying pollution with it. This cleans the air above cities. During a thermal inversion, cool air is near the ground and is trapped by warm air above. Cool air does not rise above warm air, keeping pollution down.

Water Resources

Nearly three quarters of the earth's surface is covered with water. In certain spots, each of the five oceans is miles deep. Frozen water forms polar icecaps and, at high elevations, snow covers the peaks of mountains. Water is a principle resource. Without it, we would not be able to live.

The water supply of the earth does not change. It only moves from place to place. A glass of water that you drink today may contain molecules that were used to wash a camel in Egypt thousands of years ago.

Water Zones. The United States' total supply of water is large, but some areas of our country have limited resources. In general, natural water supplies are greater in the East. Farms and cities in the western part of the nation have to use groundwater or aquifers, or transport water from one place to another.

Damaged Supplies. Pollution from sewage, industrial chemicals, fertilizers, and landfill leaks cuts down on our natural water supply by making it unfit to use. Even street litter pollutes our waters. By cutting down on wastes, we can reduce water spoilage. We can conserve water by using it carefully.

DID YOU KNOW?

- Up to one–fifth of our fresh water leaks through cracked seals and pipes on its way to the faucet.
- It takes up to 50 gallons of water to do one load of wash.
- Six percent of all the people in the United States drink bottled water to avoid pollution.
- Each person in the U.S. uses an average of 70 gallons of water each day.
- A two-minute shower uses 24 gallons of water.

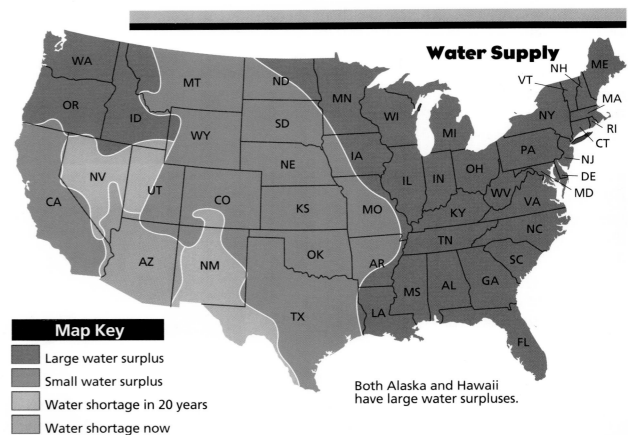

Water Supply

Map Key

- Large water surplus
- Small water surplus
- Water shortage in 20 years
- Water shortage now

Both Alaska and Hawaii have large water surpluses.

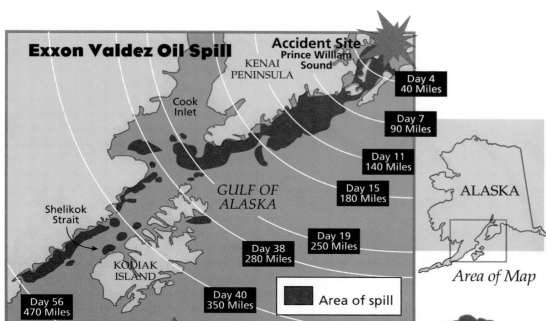

Exxon Valdez Oil Spill

Accident Site
Prince William Sound

KENAI PENINSULA

Cook Inlet

Day 4
40 Miles

Day 7
90 Miles

Day 11
140 Miles

Day 15
180 Miles

GULF OF ALASKA

Shelikok Strait

Day 19
250 Miles

Day 38
280 Miles

KODIAK ISLAND

Day 40
350 Miles

Day 56
470 Miles

Area of spill

ALASKA

Area of Map

The Exxon Valdez oil spill which occurred off the coast of Alaska in 1989 was one of many tanker accidents in our country's history. Oil flows into the water when these giant carriers are damaged. Accidents on drilling platforms spill oil into the water, too. Even more harm is done by people cleaning tankers illegally. Oil spills poison plants and animals. Birds cannot fly or feed themselves when oil coats their feathers. Spilled oil turns beautiful beaches into black pools. After the Exxon spill, thousands of workers spent months cleaning the shore and wildlife.

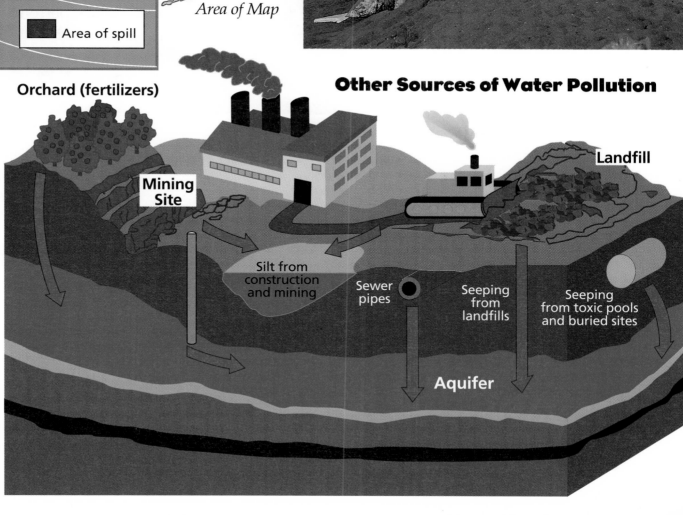

Other Sources of Water Pollution

Orchard (fertilizers)

Mining Site

Landfill

Silt from construction and mining

Sewer pipes

Seeping from landfills

Seeping from toxic pools and buried sites

Aquifer

Acid Rain and Snow

Water in the earth's atmosphere travels along the paths followed by air currents. As water vapor moves across the country, it mixes with exhausts from cars and factory smokestacks. These pollutants change water vapor into acid that sometimes is as strong as vinegar.

When polluted water vapor condenses, it falls to earth as **acid rain** or snow. Acid rain kills fish eggs in lakes and ponds. It also hurts trees, plants, and farm crops.

Recent tests show that about four percent of lakes cannot support fish any longer. Another five percent have been damaged. Small lakes and ponds can be repaired by adding large amounts of **alkalines**, like baking soda or limestone. But that is a short–term cure. A better solution is to control the pollution that causes acid rain.

How Acid Rain Is Made

Nitric oxide and sulfur dioxide combine with water vapor to form sulfuric acid (H_2SO_4) and nitric acid (HNO_3).

H_2SO_4 and HNO_3 dissolves in rain and snow.

Factories emit nitric oxide (NO) and sulfur dioxide (SO_2).

Cars emit nitric oxide (NO).

Acid rain falls to earth.

Acid Rain

Wind above the United States moves west to east and upwards to New England and Canada.

Map Key

pH 4.3 — pH 4.5 — pH 4.7 — pH 4.9 — pH 5.1

Note: Alaska and Hawaii do not have acid rain problems.

Acidity is measured on a pH scale. The lower the number, the stronger the acid. Each step is ten times stronger than the one above it.

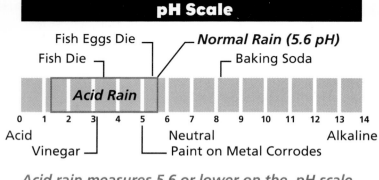

pH Scale

Fish Eggs Die — *Normal Rain (5.6 pH)*

Fish Die — Baking Soda

Acid Rain

| 0 | 1 | 2 | 3 | 4 | 5 | 6 | 7 | 8 | 9 | 10 | 11 | 12 | 13 | 14 |

Acid — Neutral — Alkaline

Vinegar — Paint on Metal Corrodes

Acid rain measures 5.6 or lower on the pH scale. Sometimes acids fall from the sky undiluted by rain. We call this acid deposition.

Draining the Rivers

The demand for water in the United States has caused real problems in many parts of the country. This is especially true in Southern California, Arizona and New Mexico, where many people have moved to enjoy the warm, sunny weather.

While the weather is comfortable in the Southwest, there are not enough natural water supplies to support large populations. Places like San Diego, California, use water much faster than the earth can give it back.

Whose Water? Faced with short supplies, Southern Californians must look elsewhere for water in order to irrigate their huge farms. The once mighty Colorado River that separates Arizona from California looked like a good source. Today, aqueducts carry water 800 miles from the river in Arizona to California's crops.

Just a Stream. People in Arizona are not happy about this arrangement. Arizona's relatively small population needs water, too. Over the years, many court battles have been fought over the water in the Colorado River. While California and Arizona debated the issue, the river has been drained. The water flow is so reduced that the river can barely complete its journey through the Grand Canyon to the Gulf of California in the south.

Draining the Colorado River

The Colorado River carved the Grand Canyon over millions of years. Today, it is a stream that has only a fraction of its earlier power or water flow. The Colorado is being drained by people in California, who need water for farming in a desert climate.

Your family can save water by...

- not watering lawns during the hot hours of the day. If you water your lawn in the evening, more water will soak into the roots of the grass and less will evaporate into the air due to the heat of the sun.

- checking the plumbing in your home. Plumbing leaks waste thousands of gallons of water each year. One drippy faucet alone will waste 10,000 gallons each and every year.

- using water-saving devices such as shower heads, toilets, and faucets. Also, most washing machines have different settings for load size. Smaller load settings use less water in the wash tub.

- brushing your teeth and doing the dishes with the water turned off. Such activities, if done with the water on, can waste thousands of gallons a year.

- washing your car with a bucket rather than a running hose. Nearly 200 gallons of water flow into the street when the hose runs.

Wetlands

An acre of wetland has as much life as an acre of tropical rainforest. Most of our freshwater fish are born and live in wetlands. One third of all our nation's birds and half of our shellfish live there, too. Wetlands are home to one out of three of all endangered species in the nation.

Paved Over. Often thought of as swamps or breeding grounds for mosquitos, wetlands have been filled in with dirt and made into sites for shopping centers and airports. Only recently have people understood how wetlands protect our environment. Working as huge filters, these areas clean polluted water before it seeps down into underground drinking supplies. They provide protection and food for countless species of plants and animals.

Fewer by the Hour. As much as eighty percent of the original wetlands in the United States are gone today. Sixty more acres are destroyed every hour. Those that remain are threatened by further development.

The U.S. government is now trying to protect the remaining wetlands. In the past two decades, these natural areas have been carefully mapped using aerial photography. Since 1985, the Swampbuster Program has discouraged farmers from draining wetlands to grow more crops.

Cranberries are a favorite food on many Thanksgiving tables. Most are grown in New England and in New Jersey. Cranberries take a lot of water to harvest. They grow best in wetland areas where water is in plentiful supply.

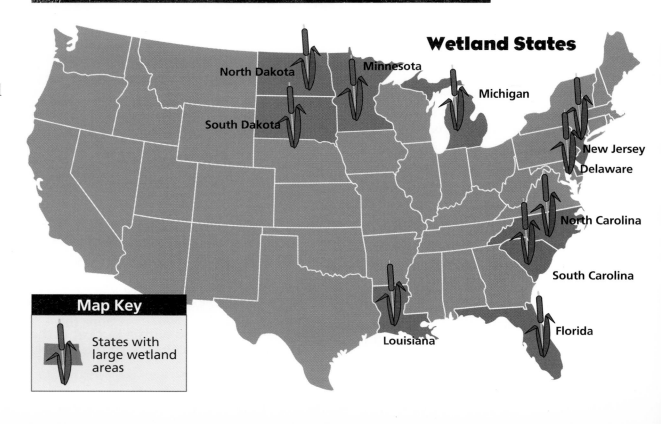

Wetland States

North Dakota

Minnesota

Michigan

South Dakota

New Jersey

Delaware

North Carolina

South Carolina

Florida

Louisiana

Map Key

States with large wetland areas

Focus: Saving the Florida Everglades

Each year, tens of thousands of visitors come to Florida's wetlands, the Everglades. Here they can see alligators, panthers, egrets, and herons—and other species not found anywhere else on earth.

Almost Lost. Most visitors don't realize that they are lucky to see anything at all. Nearly half of the Everglades are gone. For years, the waters that fed them were rerouted to provide water for drinking, recreation, and agriculture in central Florida. In 1983, Florida started the Save Our Everglades program. Scientists and environmentalists worked with the state governor to improve water quality and protect the remaining wetlands.

Farm Damage. One of the big issues was Lake Okeechobee, one of the water sources of the Everglades. Okeechobee, like many lakes in America, was suffering from nitrogen runoff from farm fertilizers. The Everglades program got the farmers to reduce the amount of nitrogen used on their land.

The program also limited the pumping of water from the wetlands. The remaining Everglades and their exotic animal and plant life were given some protection. Keeping them safe in the future will show how well people and government can work together to save our limited resources.

South Florida is home to many endangered species. Florida's people have taken five steps to protect the wetland habitats in their unique state. Their plan started by restoring the Kissimmee River, the source of water that flows south to restore the Big Cypress, and the Everglades.

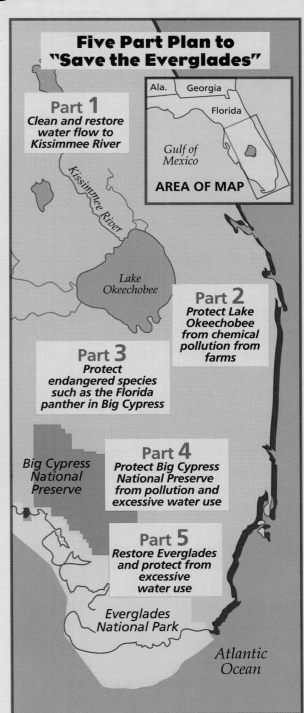

Five Part Plan to "Save the Everglades"

Part 1
Clean and restore water flow to Kissimmee River

Ala. Georgia
Florida
Gulf of Mexico
AREA OF MAP

Kissimmee River

Lake Okeechobee

Part 2
Protect Lake Okeechobee from chemical pollution from farms

Part 3
Protect endangered species such as the Florida panther in Big Cypress

Big Cypress National Preserve

Part 4
Protect Big Cypress National Preserve from pollution and excessive water use

Part 5
Restore Everglades and protect from excessive water use

Everglades National Park

Atlantic Ocean

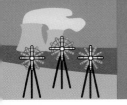

My Environment

Americans are the world's greatest consumers. The United States uses more resources per person than any country on earth. People in other countries often admire our standard of living. Other people think that we use too many resources, with little concern for the planet's future.

Use and Pollution. The U.S. uses much more energy than it produces, and more than any other country. **Fossil fuels**— such as oil, gasoline, and coal— also pollute the air and water, destroy croplands, and cause health problems.

Taking Care. We must learn to conserve the earth's natural resources so that they will not run out completely. Also, we must look at new fuels that will be less harmful to our one and only home.

In the United States, people have begun to see that the environment is not something we can afford to waste. Governments have begun to pass laws to protect our resources from misuse and pollution. Although there is sometimes resistance, more and more people understand that these laws protect all of us. They are necessary to ensure our environment for the future.

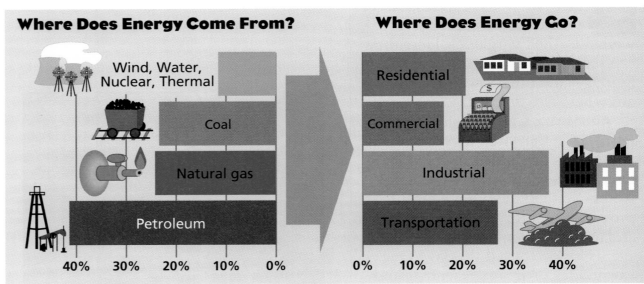

Where Does Energy Come From?

Wind, Water, Nuclear, Thermal

Coal

Natural gas

Petroleum

40% 30% 20% 10% 0%

Where Does Energy Go?

Residential

Commercial

Industrial

Transportation

0% 10% 20% 30% 40%

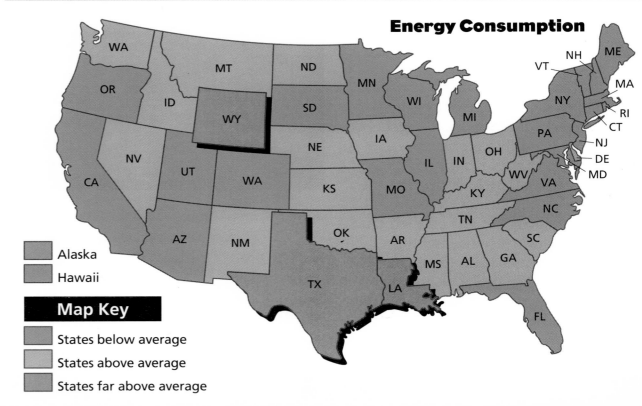

Energy Consumption

Alaska

Hawaii

Map Key

States below average

States above average

States far above average

Energy Consumed by People in Different Parts of the World

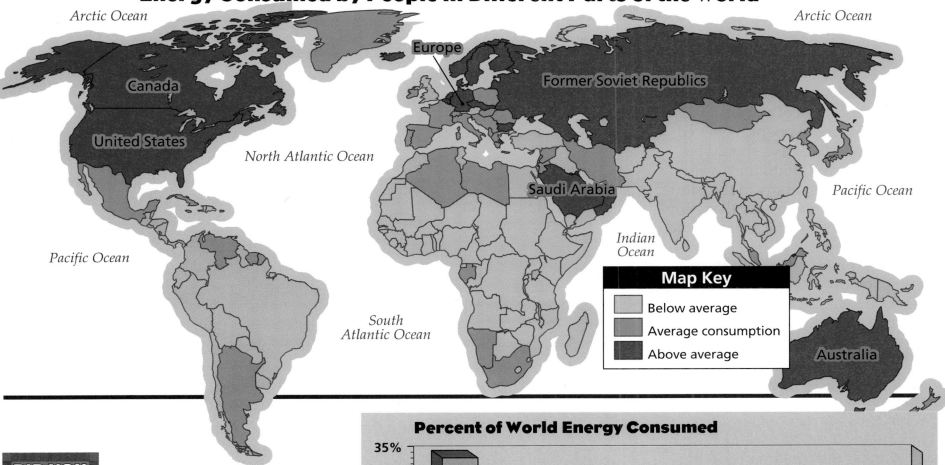

Arctic Ocean

Arctic Ocean

Canada

United States

North Atlantic Ocean

Pacific Ocean

South Atlantic Ocean

Europe

Former Soviet Republics

Saudi Arabia

Indian Ocean

Pacific Ocean

Australia

Map Key

	Below average
	Average consumption
	Above average

DID YOU KNOW ?

- The United States has only 5% of the world's people, but uses 34% of the world's energy.

- Industry consumes 36% of all U.S. energy; transportation 28%, and residents 21%.

- Texas produces the most oil and natural gas, and Kentucky produces the most coal.

- We import 70% of the oil we use from other countries.

- More than 24 million new and used cars are sold here each year.

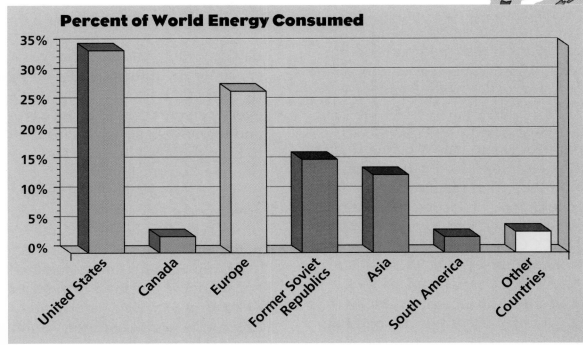

Percent of World Energy Consumed

Y-axis: 0% to 35%

Categories: United States, Canada, Europe, Former Soviet Republics, Asia, South America, Other Countries

The Environmental Movement

Much of our treasured national parks and forests were set aside by the efforts of conservationists in the 1900s. These people believed that resources like trees should be saved (conserved) until they were needed for the economy in the future. It was not until much later that people thought to save natural areas for their beauty.

Creating Jobs. During the Great Depression of the 1930s, people started to change their ideas about wilderness resources. A second conservation movement started. People needed jobs, and President Franklin Delano Roosevelt decided that the nation's land offered opportunities to put people back to work.

Under Roosevelt's leadership, the government reshaped parts of the natural landscape. Government programs, such as the Tennessee Valley Authority (TVA) and the Civilian Conservation Corps (CCC), put people and land together to bring hope to a depressed nation. The TVA built dams that ran electrical generators. These projects brought electricity and jobs to poor farmlands. The CCC put unemployed people to work building public projects, such as nature trails, roads, and bridges.

A New Movement. By the 1960s, a new movement, **environmentalism**,

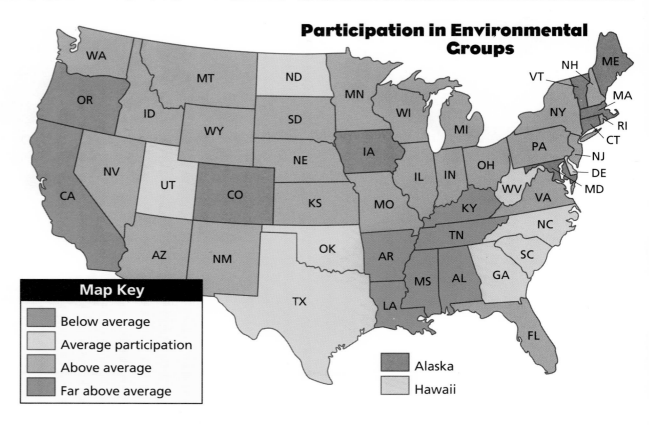

Participation in Environmental Groups

Map Key
- Below average
- Average participation
- Above average
- Far above average

Alaska
Hawaii

had started. It was based on peoples' concerns about the quality of life on the planet. Environmentalism offers every person a chance to get involved and to understand what we all can do to keep the earth healthy. Unlike previous efforts, it is not a government program. But it includes urging government leaders to make laws to protect people's health and the nation's ecosystems.

World Concern. Environmentalism has become a worldwide movement. Increasingly, people have realized that care for the earth's environment must

be shared. In 1992, 178 countries sent representatives to the world's first Earth Summit in Rio de Janeiro, Brazil.

The United States was one of 143 nations that signed a treaty to curb the use of greenhouse gases that are contributing to global warming. But it refused to sign another treaty through which countries would share research and technology in order to protect endangered species. Environmental leaders in our country and throughout the world are hoping the U. S. will cooperate more with other nations to address global problems.

Investing in the Environment

The United States has one of the richest environments on the planet. We have many resources of land, water, wildlife, and people.

Many people want us to use our resources more wisely. Recent polls suggest that they would even be willing to have their taxes raised to pay for it. There are many things the government can do with tax dollars to improve the environment, if people are willing.

Making the Difference. But government is only one part of the solution. Alone and together, people can solve many environmental problems. Some have already started environmental revolutions in their homes, schools, and offices. They recycle trash. They use less electricity, heat, and water. They plant trees. They spend a little bit extra for products that are environmentally safe.

All across the country, people are changing what is important to them. While they can't clean up toxic waste dumps without government help, they can make a dramatic difference by recycling municipal wastes and conserving other resources.

Learn More. In the back of this book are sources that you can use to start your own environmental program.

Americans are buying more "green products," which are less damaging to the environment. They include products with few artificial colors and biodegradable packaging.

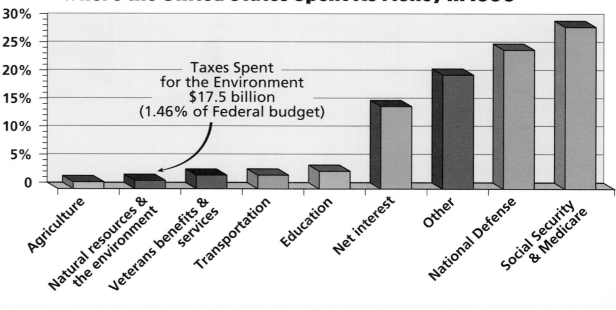

Where the United States Spent Its Money in 1990

Taxes Spent
for the Environment
$17.5 billion
(1.46% of Federal budget)

Agriculture · Natural resources & the environment · Veterans benefits & services · Transportation · Education · Net interest · Other · National Defense · Social Security & Medicare

65

Focus: Pollution in the Home

We think of pollution as something that happens in the air, or the rivers, or underground. But pollution can be as close as our own living room. The good news is that home pollution problems are some of the easiest to solve.

Creating Pollution. Our homes get polluted the same way our natural environment does. We add unhealthy or unnatural substances to them. Fumes from tobacco smoke or strong cleaning products can damage the air quality. Some of the things we do to conserve energy, such as sealing windows and adding insulation, can actually make this kind of indoor pollution worse, since air doesn't circulate easily.

Old pipes and bad plumbing systems can make water unsafe to drink. Lead used in old wall paint can be harmful to people, especially children. Old insulation, like asbestos fibers, can hurt our lungs.

The Radon Problem. Other home pollution comes from nature. **Radon**, an odorless, colorless gas, may come from the ground and pollute the home environment. Fortunately, a simple test can detect radon, and homeowners can protect themselves against its effects.

Like most environmental problems, home pollution can be greatly reduced once we become aware of its causes.

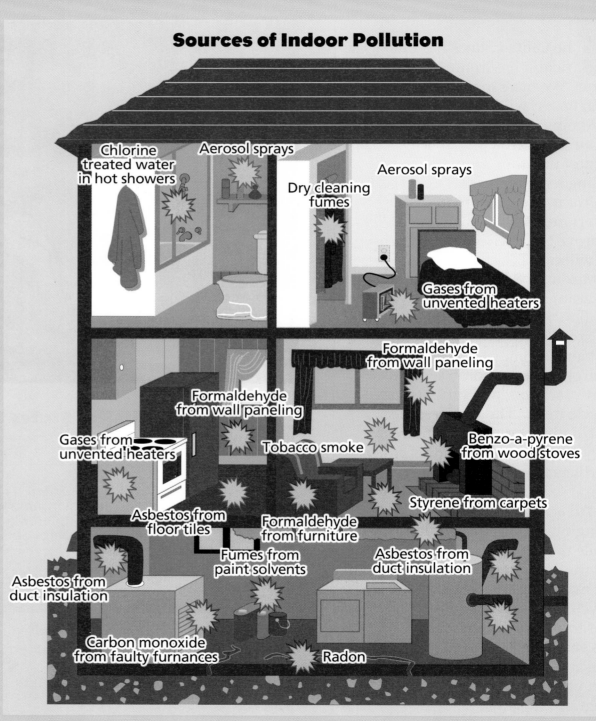

Sources of Indoor Pollution

Chlorine treated water in hot showers

Aerosol sprays

Dry cleaning fumes

Aerosol sprays

Gases from unvented heaters

Formaldehyde from wall paneling

Formaldehyde from wall paneling

Gases from unvented heaters

Tobacco smoke

Benzo-a-pyrene from wood stoves

Styrene from carpets

Asbestos from floor tiles

Formaldehyde from furniture

Asbestos from duct insulation

Fumes from paint solvents

Asbestos from duct insulation

Carbon monoxide from faulty furnances

Radon

Books to Read

ANIMALS

Macmillan Animal Encyclopedia for Children. Roger Few. Macmillan Publishing Co. 1991.

The Checkerboard Press Nature Encyclopedia. Donald M. Silver and Patricia J. Wynne. Checkerboard Press. 1990.

The Usborne Living World Encyclopedia. Leslie Colvin and Emma Speare. EDC Publishing. 1992.

THE EARTH

Earth. The Making, Shaping and Workings of a Planet. Derek Elsom. Macmillan Publishing Co. 1992.

Earthquakes. Seymour Simon. Morrow Books. 1991.

Finding Out About Our Earth. Jane Chisholm. EDC Publishing. 1991.

Geography Encyclopedia. Continents, Countries, and Peoples of the World. Checkerboard Press. 1989.

How the Earth Works. John Farndon. Dorling Kindersley Ltd. 1992.

How Nature Works. David Burnie. Dorling Kindersley Ltd. 1991.

Our Global Greenhouse. April Koral. Franklin Watts. 1990.

The Story Of the Earth. Stuart Malin. Troll. 1991.

The Usborne Book of Earth Facts. Lynn Bresler. EDC Publishing. 1986.

EARTH HISTORY

Dinosaur. David Norman and Angela Milner. Alfred A. Knopf Eyewitness Books. 1989.

Dinosaurs And Other Extinct Animals. Gabriel Beaufay. Barrons Educational Series Inc. 1987.

Early Humans. Alfred A. Knopf Eyewitness Books. 1989.

Fossil. Alfred A. Knopf Eyewitness Books. 1990.

The Evolution Book. Sara Stein. Workman Publishing. 1986.

The Great Dinosaur Atlas. William Lindsay, illustrat-ed by Guiliano Fornari. Simon and Schuster, Inc. 1991.

ENVIRONMENT

Acid Rain. Kathlyn Gay. Franklin Watts. 1983.

Acid Rain. A Sourcebook for Young People. Christine Miller and Louise Berry. Julian Messner. 1986.

Air Pollution. Kathlyn Gay. Franklin Watts. 1991.

Disaster. The Destruction of Our Planet. George Sullivan. Scholastic Inc. 1992.

Garbage! Where It Comes From, Where It Goes. Evan and Janet Hadijhan. Simon and Schuster Books for Young People. 1990.

FORESTS, TREES, AND PLANTS

Ancient Forests. A Celebration of North America's Old Growth Wilderness. David Middleton. Chronicle Books. 1992.

Plant. David Burnie. Alfred A. Knopf Eyewitness Books. 1989.

Rainforest Secrets. Arthur Dorros. Scholastic Inc. 1992.

Rainforests for Beginners. Naomi Rosenblatt. Writers and Readers Publishing Inc. 1992.

Rain Forest. Helen Cowcher. Farrar, Straus and Giroux. A Sunburst Book. 1991.

Tree. Alfred A. Knopf Eyewitness Books. 1989.

Tree Life. A Close Up Look at a Tree. Theresa Greenaway, photographed by Kim Taylor. Dorling Kindersley Ltd. 1992.

Tropical Rainforests Around The World. Elaine Landau. Franklin Watts. 1990.

WATER

Oceanography. Larry Wade, illustrated by Stephen Bolles. Singing Rock Press. 1992.

Oceans. Seymour Simon. Morrow Junior Books. 1990.

Pond and River. Steve Parker. Alfred A. Knopf Eyewitness Books. 1988.

River Life. Barbara Taylor, photographed by Frank Greenaway. Dorling Kindersley Ltd. 1992.

Seashore. Alfred A. Knopf Eyewitness Books. 1989.

Tide Pool. Christiane Gunzi, photographed by Frank Greenaway. Dorling Kindersley Ltd. 1992.

WEATHER AND CLIMATE

Science For Kids. 39 Easy Meteorology Experiments. Robert W. Wood. TAB Books. 1992.

Weather. Brian Cosgrove. Alfred A. Knopf Eyewitness Books. 1991.

Weather. Howard E. Smith, illustrated by Jeffrey K. Bedrick. Doubleday. 1990.

Weather and Climate. Fiona Watt and Francis Wilson. Usborne Publishing Ltd. 1992.

HELPING THE PLANET

Earth Child. Games, Stories, Activities, Experiments, and Ideas About Living Lightly On Planet Earth. Kathryn Sheehan and Mary Waidner. Council Oak Books. 1991.

50 Simple Things Kids Can Do to Save the Earth. Andrews and McMeel. The Earthworks Group, A Universal Press Syndicate Company. 1990.

I Helped Save The Earth. 55 Fun Ways Kids Can Make a World of Difference. Michael O'Brian. Berkeley Books. 1991.

Save The Earth. An Action Handbook for Kids. Betty Miles. Alfred A. Knopf. 1991.

Radon. The Citizen's Guide. Environmental Defense Fund. New York. 1992.

Teaching Kids to Love the Earth. Marina Lachecki Herman, Joseph F. Dassineau, Ann L. Schimpf, Paul Treuer. Pfeifer–Hamilton. 1991.

The City Kids Field Guide. Ethan Herberman. Simon and Schuster, Inc. 1989.

Save Our Planet. 750 Everyday Ways You Can Help Clean Up the Earth. Diane MacEachern. Dell Publishing. 1990.

The Solution to Pollution. 101 Things You Can Do to Clean Up Your Environment. Lawrence Sombke. Master Media Limited. 1990.

U.S. Facts

Compiled from U.S. Census 1990 and *The World Almanac,* 1980 and 1992.

Place	1990 Population	Rank Population	Persons Per Square Mile	Land Area (sq. miles)	Water Area (sq. miles)	Total Area (sq. miles)	Average Elevation (ft.)
United States	248,691,873	—	70	3,536,345	82,388	3,618,733	
Alabama	4,040,587	22	80	50,750	955	51,705	500
Alaska	550,043	50	1	570,373	20,627	591,000	1,900
Arizona	3,665,228	24	32	113,642	358	114,000	4,100
Arkansas	2,350,725	33	45	52,075	1,112	53,187	650
California	29,760,021	1	191	155,973	2,733	158,706	2,900
Colorado	3,294,394	26	32	103,730	361	104,091	6,800
Connecticut	3,287,116	27	678	4,845	173	5,018	500
Delaware	666,168	46	341	1,955	90	2,045	60
District of Columbia	606,900	48	9,884	63	6	69	150
Florida	12,937,926	4	240	53,997	4,667	58,664	100
Georgia	6,478,216	11	112	57,919	991	58,910	600
Hawaii	1,108,229	41	173	6,423	48	6,471	3,030
Idaho	1,006,749	42	12	82,751	813	83,564	5,000
Illinois	11,430,602	6	206	55,593	752	56,345	600
Indiana	5,544,159	14	155	35,870	315	36,185	700
Iowa	2,776,755	30	50	55,875	400	56,275	1,100
Kansas	2,477,574	32	30	81,823	454	82,277	2,000
Kentucky	3,685,296	23	93	39,732	678	40,410	750
Louisiana	4,219,973	21	97	43,566	4,186	47,752	100
Maine	1,227,928	38	40	30,865	2,400	33,265	600
Maryland	4,781,468	19	489	9,775	685	10,460	350
Massachusetts	6,016,425	13	768	7,838	446	8,284	500
Michigan	9,295,297	8	164	56,809	1,718	58,527	900
Minnesota	4,375,099	20	55	79,617	4,785	84,402	1,200
Mississippi	2,573,216	31	54	46,914	775	47,689	300

Place	1990 Population	Rank Population	Persons Per Square Mile	Land Area (sq. miles)	Water Area (sq. miles)	Total Area (sq. miles)	Average Elevation (ft.)
Missouri	5,117,073	15	74	68,898	799	69,697	800
Montana	799,065	44	6	145,556	1,490	147,046	3,400
Nebraska	1,578,385	36	21	76,878	477	77,355	2,600
Nevada	1,201,833	39	11	109,806	755	110,561	5,500
New Hampshire	1,109,252	40	124	8,969	310	9,279	1,000
New Jersey	7,730,188	9	1,042	7,419	368	7,787	250
New Mexico	1,515,069	37	13	121,364	229	121,593	5,700
New York	17,990,455	2	381	47,224	1,884	49,108	1,000
North Carolina	6,628,637	10	136	48,718	3,951	52,669	700
North Dakota	638,800	47	9	68,994	1,708	70,702	1,900
Ohio	10,847,115	7	265	40,953	377	41,330	850
Oklahoma	3,145,585	28	46	68,679	1,240	69,919	1,300
Oregon	2,842,321	29	30	96,003	1,070	97,073	3,300
Pennsylvania	11,881,643	5	265	44,820	488	45,308	1,100
Rhode Island	1,003,464	43	960	1,045	167	1,212	200
South Carolina	3,468,703	25	116	30,111	1,002	31,113	350
South Dakota	696,004	45	9	75,898	1,218	77,116	2,200
Tennessee	4,877,185	17	118	41,220	924	42,144	900
Texas	16,986,510	3	65	261,914	4,893	266,807	1,700
Utah	1,722,850	35	21	82,168	2,731	84,899	6,100
Vermont	562,758	49	61	9,249	365	9,614	1,000
Virginia	6,187,358	12	156	39,598	1,169	40,767	950
Washington	4,866,692	18	73	66,582	1,557	68,139	1,700
West Virginia	1,793,477	34	75	24,087	145	24,232	1,500
Wisconsin	4,891,769	16	90	54,314	1,839	56,153	1,050
Wyoming	453,588	51	5	97,105	704	97,809	6,700

Where to Write

**CARETAKERS
OF THE ENVIRONMENT
INTERNATIONAL/USA**
2216 Schiller Ave.
Wilmette, IL 60091 or
13422 Stardust Blvd.
Sun City West, AZ 85375
(708) 251-8935
An international network that helps
students in places as far apart as India,
Africa, England, and the U.S., work together
on environment-related projects. Projects
include "Eco-art" in Arizona, using
horticulture to improve science education in
Chicago, and promoting peace through the
environment in Northern Ireland.

**CHILDREN'S ALLIANCE FOR PROTECTION
OF THE ENVIRONMENT (CAPE)**
P.O. Box 307
Austin, TX 78767
(512) 476-2273
A global children's network that has
information about hands-on projects,
including beach and lake shore cleanups,
tree-planting, preservation of rainforests
and animal habitats, and waste disposal. Its
newspaper, written by kids, is called "Many
Hands."

EARTH KIDS ORGANIZATION
P.O. Box 3847
Salem, OR 97302
(503) 363-1896
A school-based computer network set up to
communicate environmental information
and the results of projects, such as adopting
streams, animals, and trees.

EARTH TRAIN
99 Brookwood Rd., Suite 3
Orinda, CA 94563
(510) 254-9101

Has a ten-year Global Campaign using peer
seminars to encourage student commitment
to the environment and to community
service in the U.S., Europe, and Japan.

ENVIRONMENTAL YOUTH ALLIANCE
P.O. Box 34097, Station D
Vancouver, B.C. V6J 4M1, CANADA
(604) 737-2258
Works to address such concerns as the
protection of ancient forests, ozone
depletion, and stewardship of Canadian
land.

THE GIRAFFE PROJECT
197 Second St., P.O. Box 759
Langley, Whidbey Island, WA 98260
(206) 221-7989
"A press agency for heroes" that collects
and publishes stories about kids who work
to improve the earth.

GROUND TRUTH STUDIES PROJECT
The Aspen Global Change Institute
100 East Francis
Aspen, CO 81611
(303) 925-7376
Conducts hands-on projects using remote
sensing and satellite images of local
environments. Its goal is to help kids
understand that events in their local
environment are related to global
environmental change.

KIDS AGAINST POLLUTION (K.A.P.)
P.O. Box 775
Closter, NJ 07624
(201) 784-0668
Organizes environmental campaigns, town
clean-ups, recycling programs, and has
written an environmental Bill of Rights with
federal and state sponsorship.

THE KIDS' EARTH WORKS GROUP
1400 Shattuck Ave., #25
Berkeley, CA 94709
Distributes information on the environment
and publishes "Sources for Young
Environmentalists," a list which directs kids
to groups that concentrate on their specific
questions.

**KIDS FOR A CLEAN ENVIRONMENT
(KIDS FACE)**
P.O. Box 158254
Nashville, TN 37215
(615) 331-7381
Conducts letter-writing and hands-on
projects to encourage world leaders to help
stop pollution. FACE started with one kid
who got her unanswered letter to the
President displayed on several billboards.

KIDS FOR CONSERVATION
Illinois Dept. of Conservation
524 S. Second St.
Springfield, IL 62701
(217) 524-4126
The kid's branch of the Illinois Dept. of
Conservation which distributes a state-wide
newsletter about conservation of natural
resources.

KIDS FOR SAVING EARTH (KSE)
P.O. Box 47247
Plymouth, MN 55447-0247
(612) 525-0002
Encourages rainforest adoption, creating
"backyard habitats," adopting endangered
animals, and education through petitions,
plays, and its newspaper.

KIDS IN NATURE'S DEFENSE CLUBS (KIND)
P.O. Box 362
East Haddam, CT 06423-0362
(203) 434-8666
Publishes KIND News, which promotes kindness to animals, people, and the earth. Subscriptions and information on projects, including environmental protection and pet overpopulation, are available.

KIDS NETWORK
National Geographic Society
Educational Services, Dept. 1001
Washington, DC 20077
(800) 368-2728
Conducts computerized classes that allow students to communicate with other students about topics such as acid rain and water pollution.

KIDS RENEW AMERICA
1400 16th Street. NW, Suite 710
Washington, DC 20036
(202) 232-2252
A clearinghouse for collected success stories about kids who have contributed to a better environment.

THE NATURAL GUARD (T.N.G.)
2631 Durham Rd.
Guilford, CT 06437
A service organization whose activities include pollution patrols, tree planting, and urban trail-building.

PROJECT WILD
P.O. Box 18060
Boulder, CO 80308-8060
(303) 444-2390
Suggests activities for teachers and their classes which focus on the importance of habitat and the effects of human activity on wildlife.

SOIL AND WATER CONSERVATION SOCIETY (SWCS)
7515 NE Ankeney Rd.
Ankeney, IA 50021-9764
(515) 289-2331
Concerned with land and water quality and conservation. It publishes "Water in Your Hands," "Make Room for Monsters and Wildlife on the Land," and other comic books about human relationships with the natural world.

STUDENT CONSERVATION ASSOCIATION (SCA)
P.O. Box 550
Charlestown, NH 03603-0550
(603) 826-4301
Helps students get summer jobs and volunteer work in stewardships of public lands and natural resources. Also offers outdoor experiences for developmentally or learning-disabled, or at-risk kids.

STUDENT ENVIRONMENTAL ACTION COALITION (SEAC)
P.O. Box 1168
Chapel Hill, NC 27514-1168
(919) 967-4600
Aims to unify student activists, through a national support group, to deal with environmental issues ranging from recycling to toxic disposal. Concentrates on social reasons for environmental problems.

SUPER KIDS RECYCLING PROGRAM
P.O. Box 242
Iselin, NJ 08830
This group will send you an activity package for drawing and making posters from waste materials that haven't been used yet. It also tells you how you can re-use everyday objects.

TREE AMIGOS
Center for Environmental Study
143 Bostwick NE
Grand Rapids, MI 49503
(616) 771-3935
Kids from Costa Rica and the U.S. raise funds to buy and protect tropical forests, to recycle paper, and to plant trees. Seeks to increase cross-cultural communication through shared protection of the global environment.

YOUTH FOR ENVIRONMENTAL SANITY (YES!)
706 Frederick St.
Santa Cruz, CA 95062
(408) 459-9344
Conducts workshops in U.S. schools that motivate kids to solve environmental problems and train them to be effective activists.

Glossary

acid rain. Rain that is polluted by sulfuric acid and nitric acid formed when pollutants combine with water in the atmosphere. These acids can also pollute snow.

actual vegetation. Plants growing in a particular place, usually planted by humans. (See natural vegetation.)

air pollution. Chemicals and particles in the air that can hurt humans, animals, and plants.

alkaline. A substance having a pH level of more than 7.

alluvial soil. Soil deposited by moving water, such as a river.

altitude. Height above sea level.

ancient forests. Uncut old forests. Forests that have not been harvested by people.

aqueduct. An artificial river or channel that is built to move water from one place to another.

aquifer. Underground layers of rock and sand that hold large amounts of water.

archaeologist. A scientist who studies life in the past, often by studying objects that have been buried for a long time.

atmosphere. The gases that surround a planet. Earth's atmosphere is primarily made up of nitrogen and oxygen.

atmospheric pressure. The pressure of the earth's atmosphere.

biodegradable. Substances that can be broken down into smaller elements by bacteria. Paper and animal wastes are examples.

biodiversity. The variety of animals and plants that make up the earth's living environment.

biological community. An area where the habitats of tens, or even hundreds, of species of plants and animals overlap, and many organisms are interdependent.

biome. A major life zone of interdependent plants and animals. Deserts, rain forests, and grasslands are examples.

biosphere. The part of the earth where life can be found. It includes the air, land, and sea.

chemicals. The different solids, liquids, and gases of the earth that are made of simple elements and are either found in nature or made by people.

chlorofluorocarbons (CFCs). Organic chemical compounds used in refrigerators and air-conditioners to make things cold, and in plastic items such as Styrofoam. When burned or released into the atmosphere, CFCs are destructive to the ozone layer.

clear-cutting. The act of cutting down all the trees in a forest rather than cutting selectively.

climate. The average weather of a region measured over a long period of years.

coastal wetlands. Areas along the coast that are covered with salt water most of the year. Marshes, bays, and lagoons are examples of coastal wetlands.

compost. Plant and animal matter that has broken down or decomposed, and is used for fertilizer.

coniferous plants. Plants that reproduce through seeds carried in cones. Most are evergreen and do not lose their leaves in winter.

conservationists. People who believe in protecting natural resources from waste and destruction.

core. The intensely hot center of the earth which is made up of two parts, the solid inner core and the liquid outer core.

deciduous plants. Plants and trees that shed their leaves during the winter.

desert. A large, dry area where evaporation of water is greater than rainfall.

drought. A long period when water supplies are used faster than rain can replace them.

earthquake. The shaking of the ground due to the movement of the earth's crust.

ecology. The study of how living organisms interact with each other and the world.

economy. The system by which goods and services are produced, distributed, and used in a society. Also, the careful and efficient use of resources.

ecosystem. A community of plants and animals interacting with each other and their physical environment.

endangered species. A particular kind of plant or animal that is in danger of extinction.

energy. The power to do work.

Environmental Protection Agency (EPA). The part of the federal government that carries out the rules and regulations dealing with clean air, water, and soil.

environmentalist. A person who is working to solve problems involving the world's ecosystems.

erosion. The wearing away of soil and rock from the earth's surface through the movement of wind or water.

evaporation. To change from a liquid or solid into a vapor.

extinction. The complete disappearance of a plant or animal from the earth.

fertilizer. The man-made or natural material used to enrich soil and help plants grow.

forest. An area of trees. A forest biome can support large numbers and kinds of plants and animals.

fossil fuel. Any fuel, such as coal, oil, and natural gas, that is made from decomposed plants and/or animals.

glacier. A large area of flowing ice and snow which moves slowly outward from the center in an area where snowfall is greater than melting.

global warming. The gradual warming of the earth's climate caused by the build-up of carbon dioxide and other gases that prevent the heat given off by the earth from escaping into space.

grasslands. (See prairies).

greenhouse effect. An effect by which gases in the earth's atmosphere act like the glass windows of a greenhouse. That is, they let in the sunlight but trap some of the heat that is radiated back from the earth's surface.

greenhouse gases. The gases in the earth's atmosphere that prevent heat from escaping into space. Ozone, carbon dioxide, and CFCs are examples of greenhouse gases.

groundwater. Water that seeps into the soil after a rainstorm and is stored in an aquifer.

gully erosion. Erosion caused by fast moving water that cuts deep ditches, or gullies, in the soil.

habitat. A region where a plant or animal lives.

hazardous waste. Waste that can be dangerous to people and other living things. It can come in the form of a solid, liquid, or gas, and must be stored with great care.

hydrosphere. The water on the earth's land and in its atmosphere.

ice ages. Periods in the earth's history when the average temperature is so low that glaciers covered much of the northern parts of the planet.

incineration. The burning of solid wastes.

industrial smog. A type of air pollution that is made up of solid particles and gases released by factory processes.

insecticide. (See pesticide.)

irrigation. The watering of plants through artificial methods.

landfill. A place where solid wastes are dumped and stored in, or on top of, the ground.

landforms. Special features of the earth, such as mountains, river valleys, and canyons.

latitude. Distance north or south from the Equator, measured in degrees.

low-waste disposal. A method of controlling garbage by recycling and consuming less.

magma. Liquid or molten rock deep within the earth.

mantle. The hot, rocky area of the earth's interior between the crust and the core.

metropolitan area. A large city and its smaller surrounding communities.

minerals. Naturally occurring substances that are neither plant nor animal.

municipal waste. Garbage and other refuse created by individuals rather than industry or farming.

natural resources. All material that occurs naturally, and is used by people.

natural vegetation. The plants that grow without human cultivation in a place.

old-growth forest. (See ancient forest.)

organic farming. Agriculture that uses natural, rather than chemical, fertilizers and food.

ozone. An invisible gas that surrounds the earth at approximately twelve miles above sea level. Ozone is a form of oxygen and occurs naturally in other parts of the atmosphere.

73

perennials. Plants that have a life cycle of more than two years.

pesticide. Chemicals used to destroy insects and other living creatures not wanted in a particular area.

photosynthesis. The reaction by which plants take water and carbon dioxide and produce oxygen and carbohydrates.

pollutants. Substances that dirty the air, water, and soil.

pollution. A change in the air, water, or land that is not healthy for humans and other living organisms.

population. A number of living things of the same species living in the same general area.

prairies. Flat areas with moderate-to-poor rainfall and grassy vegetation. Also grasslands.

precipitation. Water that falls to the earth in the form of rain or snow or hail.

radiation. Fast moving waves of energy created by changes within atoms and molecules.

recycling. The collecting and reusing of material such as tin, aluminum, wood, and paper.

reservoirs. Places where water is stored.

resources. All materials that would be useful to people.

runoff. Water from rain and melting ice that flows into streams, rivers, lakes, and oceans.

rural area. An area with less than 2500 people.

secondary forest. A forest that grows in an area after old-growth forests have been removed.

sheet erosion. Water erosion over a large slope or field. This type of erosion is not as noticeable as gully erosion, because it removes soil evenly over large areas.

silviculture. The farming of trees.

smog. A compound dangerous to living things created when the sun strikes air polluted by automobiles or factories.

soil. Mixture of inorganic matter (clay, rocks, sand), organic matter (decaying plants and animals), water, and living organisms.

soil profile. Cross-section or cutaway of the soil.

solid waste. Any waste that is not liquid or gas.

species. A group of organisms that look like each other and have the same gene structure.

stratosphere. A layer in the earth's atmosphere approximately twenty-five miles above the surface.

surface runoff. Water flowing from the land to a body of water.

temperature. Amount of heat of an area, usually measured in degrees.

throw-away methods. Disposal of wastes in ways that do not conserve resources. These include landfills and incineration.

top soil. The very top layer of the soil profile. It usually contains the most nutrients and is the part of the soil first to be eroded.

toxic waste. Hazardous waste that can cause death or serious injury if not disposed of properly. See also hazardous waste.

trash-to-steam incineration. A method of burning trash that captures the heat and uses it to power electric generators.

tropical rain forests. Old-growth forests near the Equator that are home to between fifty to ninety percent of the earth's species.

troposphere. The lowest layer in the earth's atmosphere starting at sea level and rising to seven miles above the surface.

urban area. An area with a population of more than 2500 people.

vegetation. Plants as they exist in an ecosystem.

virgin forest. (See ancient forest.)

water pollution. A change in the water supply that makes it harmful to fish, humans, and other life.

weather. Short-term conditions of temperature, rainfall, wind, or cloud cover.

wetlands. Land that is covered with water for all or part of the year. Wetlands purify polluted water and provide homes for plants and animals.

Index

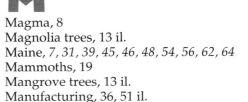